Feminism FOR REAL

Deconstructing the academic industrial complex of feminism

Edited by Jessica Yee

Fourth volume in the
Our Schools/Our Selves book series

D1403150

Feminism FOR REAL
Deconstructing the academic industrial complex of feminism
2011

Fourth volume in the *Our School/Our Selves* book series.

EXECUTIVE EDITOR
Erika Shaker

VOLUME EDITOR
Jessica Yee

EDITORIAL OFFICE
Canadian Centre for Policy Alternatives
Suite 205, 75 Albert Street, Ottawa, ON, K1P 5E7
Tel: (613) 563-1341   Fax: (613) 233-1458

ISBN 978-1-926888-49-1

PRODUCTION
Typesetting and design: Nancy Reid
Cover illustration: Jennifer Yee
Cover design: Nancy Reid (www.nrgrafix.com)

Printed in Canada by DLR International Printing, 925, boul. de la
Carriere, Gatineau, QC. Publications Mail Registration No. 8010.

Contents

DEDICATION

I would like to dedicate this book to all of my family —
biological, through ceremony, and of choice —
who always keep it real for me.

Jessica Yee

Acknowledgements

This book was a two year journey in the arms of someone who doesn't consider herself a writer at all — so I was incredibly blessed to have so much support along the way! I would like to first give thanks to my ancestors right on down the line for never giving up so that I and the next seven generations could be here today — I am here because you refused to back down no matter how hard it was. I would like to thank all the contributors to the book who are an incredibly gifted group of people who stood by me through the whole editing process and worked very closely with me to get this done: it was a mutually educational and nourishing experience. Thank you to the staff at the CCPA, especially the fabulous Erika Shaker who is jazzy and adaptable no matter what comes up and so willing to support, support, support — thank you! I would like to acknowledge the path-paving work of my Indigenous sisters Katsi Cook, Lee Maracle, Kim Anderson, Andrea Smith, Ellen Gabriel, and Beverly Jacobs — nia:wen ko:wa for what you have done for the people and communities, I wouldn't have the perspectives I have if it wasn't for your tireless work. Thank you ever so much to our amazing staff, board, and youth members of the Native Youth Sexual Health Network who have stuck through it all and give me more and more reasons every day to move forward.

Lastly I would like to say much love to all my family — biologically, in ceremony, and of choice — for believing in me and bringing me this far. Especially to my sister Jennifer, who designed the cover and is my personal source of strength and resiliency, and to my Indigenous feminist partner in crime, DJ, with whom I've finally started to find out what a healthy relationship means — and it's awesome.

JESSICA YEE

Introduction

I don't have a degree in university.

There, I said it. Phew. It's out in the open. In the printed word. No matter what I say or allude to, I just admitted I did not graduate from university — although it's true I went for about three months … and then I left. So now I hope you will continue to read this — even if I did just drop a few points on the intelligence scale of where you might have thought I was — if you happen to have such a scale. It was important for me to be truthful from the onset. And I didn't think I needed a university degree to put this book together anyway.

Before I continue, I'd like to share two points of clarification about this book:

- It is not a hate-on of academia.
- It is not a hate-on of feminism.

In fact this book is what I would call some "truth-telling"; truth-telling about some uncomfortable truths. One of my favourite quotes from Mohawk scholar Taiaiake Alfred goes: "There needs to be struggle in order to lay out a path to co-existence, and that the process of being uncomfortable is essential for non-Indigenous peoples to move from being enemy, to adversary, to ally." I think this book has some of that in there — not just in reference to Indigenous peoples, but in regard to the uncomfortable work that needs to be done by everyone if we are to have any hope of changing the effects of hundreds and hundreds of years of colonization and genocide that led us to the oppressions and inequities alive and well today that feminism is supposed to be "fixing".

However we're not really equal when we're STILL supposed to uncritically and obediently cheer when white women are praised for winning "women's rights," and to painfully forget the Indigenous women and women of colour who were hurt in that same process. We are not equal when in the name of "feminism", so-called "women's only" spaces are created and get to police and regulate who is and isn't a "woman" based on *their* interpretation of your body parts and gender presentation, not your own. We are not equal when initiatives to achieve gender equity have reverted yet again to "saving" people and making decisions for them, rather than supporting their right to self-determination, whether it's engaging in sex work, or wearing a niqab. So when feminism itself has become its own form of oppression, what do we have to say about it? Western notions of polite discourse are not the norm for all of us, and just because we've got some new and hot language like "intersectionality" to use in our talk, it doesn't necessarily make things change in our walk (i.e., actually *being* anti-racist). And I have to say that these uncomfortable processes have been worth the many paths that brought the different contributors of the book together to tell their sometimes uncomfortable truths — not just about feminism, but about themselves and where they are coming from.

Onondaga Chief Oren Lyons said it best: "If you are going to take a stand for our people, know that you are probably going to get shot in the back by arrows from over 200 years of colonization and oppression. You gotta be prepared for that." When I listened to him say that this past April 2010 at the ninth session of the United Nations Permanent Forum on Indigenous Issues I felt like he was speaking directly to me — and, moreover, that I *needed* to hear what he was saying. So much of my own identity in the work that I'm involved in across Turtle Island (what is now known as "North America") has been wrapped up in trying to measure up to being a "good" feminist, even though it was never just about "women's rights" for me — in my life I never had the option for it to be just about that, even if I tried. But now I'm going to take a stand and say that I'm constantly questioning what feminism even is, and I'm increasingly disturbed every day by the gate-keeping of who and what gets to decide the answer to that question.

So here's another truth about me: I'm at a point in my activism where in many spaces I no longer feel comfortable just saying that I'm a feminist, full-stop, without adding a few words before or after. I say I'm a multi-racial Indigenous Two-Spirit feminist. I say I'm a hip-hop feminist, a reproductive justice feminist. Like many people, I feel like I've been burned out by the mainstream usage and representation of feminism and I'm not making any apologies for what I call myself, because I'm speaking the English language of the colonizer, and if it takes people a few extra words to give me my right to self-determination of what I want to be called in English, so be it. Being uncomfortable with this truth about feminism helps keep my fire alive to change it, and also helps me to not forget where we've really come from and where we're really going.

My hope for this book is that while withstanding and fighting back against those arrows of colonization and oppression Oren was talking about, we would also take apart, or "deconstruct" what has led to the existence of "feminism" in the first place, and where feminism exists today. I wanted to learn about people's understandings and experiences of feminism in real life and go deeper than the notion that it just exists within the walls of the academy — in big textbooks, universities and colleges, or other fancy institutions. Not because I now hate academia, but because I've lost count of the amount of times I've been asked by others — and asked myself the question that is now the main title of this book, "But what *is* feminism, for real?"

The responses I received when putting this very question out there to create the book demonstrated resoundingly that people did want to talk about this notion of "the academic industrial complex of feminism" — the conflicts between what feminism means at school as opposed to at home, the frustrations of trying to relate to definitions of feminism that will never fit no matter how much you try to change yourself to fit them, and the anger and frustration of changing a system while being in the system yourself.

Last summer of June 2010 I shared the idea of this book with a dear friend and colleague Andrea Carmen, from the Yaqui nation, who is the Executive Director of the International Indian Treaty Council and the first woman to ever be in this position. We were driving to Alamo, California for the first International Indigenous Women's Environmental and Reproductive Justice Symposium when, upon hearing that I was putting this book together, she told me that she got her start in this work after completing a Women's Studies degree at the University of California, Santa Cruz.

And after hearing her tell me this story, that's when I knew for sure that this isn't just about feminism, academia, or even the book itself. It's about so much more.

Andrea Carmen: Well, it's interesting that you are talking about this, Jessica, because I graduated with a degree in Women's Studies.

Jessica Yee: What?! Really?

AC: Yes, I was part of the Women's Studies Collective at UCSC. The collective actually ran the Women's Studies department. We decided the budget, what we wanted to see as the curriculum, and which professors we wanted to hire. There were also no "grades" per se either — your professors had to write a report where they were connecting with and valuing the work you were doing.

JY: Wait, wait, wait. There was such thing as a collective actually RUNNING a Women's Studies department? Where students got to have an actual say in the education they were receiving before they got it?!

AC: Yes, there was a student advisor in addition to members of the collective steering committee. We hired people like Angela Davis, Women of All Red Nations (WARN) — I mean, we got to bring in really amazing groups of women.

JY: OMG, things like that don't even exist anymore. I mean, not to that extent that you are talking about.

AC: Actually every time I run into a current student at UCSC and I tell them about my experience at UCSC and the Women's Studies Collective, they don't believe it.

JY: Tell me about it!

AC: My reason for getting involved as a college student was because at that time in the 70s it was just coming out that Indian Health Service was sterilizing Indigenous women as a matter of United States government policy. We found out for example that Claremore in Oklahoma was one of the biggest institutions where it was taking place; it was happening in South Dakota, and all over. It was actual state policy to sterilize an Indigenous woman, including during childbirth, while under anaesthesia, or with the threat of other children being taken away, or welfare being cut off. I mean, there are so many stories of how it happened.

I actually experienced a similar kind of thing myself when I was in surgery at Stanford hospital which is a teaching university hospital. So a lot of this information was just coming out of our real lived experiences, and we wanted to form the Coalition Against Sterilization Abuse (CASA) to take action against it. We were able to find space to host awareness events, and get university credits by the Women's Collective to do this work.

JY: Wow, wow, wow. So this is where it all started for you, then, the concept of Free, Prior, and Informed Consent (FPIC)?

AC: When I first heard of FPIC, to me it was about medical procedures, something we won with the exposure and cessation of sterilization as government policy. FPIC in this instance means you have the right to feel fully informed (while awake) and to hear the pros and cons, the right to have a waiting period if you want it, and the right to hear about other options to sterilization that aren't forever — like birth control.

It's a really interesting history how it became central to our work and recognition of our rights as Indigenous peoples — the right to FPIC now relating to development on our territories, our laws, to toxins being used on our lands, to cultural items, and it all started as medical term. It started with the right of women to say yes or no, to be fully awake and not under threat when they give their agreement to any kind of medication.

JY: So people were really supportive of this in your department?

AC: At the time I resisted calling this a feminist issue — people in our department were saying this was a "women's rights" issue. I said no this is not a "women's issue" — it's a genocide issue. It happens to be something that is happening predominantly to women, yes, but we are really talking about genocide of our people as a whole.

It's interesting that today we work a lot with the United Nations Declaration on the Rights of Indigenous People and FPIC is literally the hardest fought principle that we have been pushing for. In the United States' so-called "endorsement" of the Declaration this past year, this is a clear item they are resisting because they are saying it's up to their "interpretation" of our rights by doing "consultation". Which is of course completely different, consultation is a meeting — consent means the right to say no or yes with whatever conditions you want to put.

JY: What did you think about feminism back then?

AC: I'm going to speak frankly. I think of it as a white woman's movement. This was certainly the case when I first became familiar with the term and the "ism" white women identified with. Those of us who were Native American and Chicano women at UCSC felt isolated by that philosophy which seemed to be something that pit male against female, with the primary oppressor being the man. We came to realize that maybe for white women it was the white male that was the oppressor in their culture — but for us as Indigenous peoples it was the entire colonizer and colonizing society, and the male-female subdivision was not a predominant focus. It took time, sharing, and understanding for us to be part of a collective that identified with feminism rather than anti-colonialism or Indigenous rights.

It was always an interesting discussion and opportunity to discuss with them how, for example, in our communities we refuse to see the oppression only being perpetrated by men. Our men have been affected by colonization — we aren't saying we don't see the violence against women committed by men, or rape, or domestic violence. However we see that in a bigger context — we don't see "men" to be the single primary enemy.

JY: I'm continuously intrigued by the siloing and compartmentalizing of feminism — as you mentioned before, what gets considered "feminist" issues, what doesn't, and by whom.

AC: We listened to white women speak a lot — there were some white women from poor and working class backgrounds who also put a class and economic spin in the primary ways they identified their struggles in their wage for justice. Some of them said they sometimes see the upper class white women as being more oppressive than the men. There is a lot of different shading and different ways to look at it.

Something that was always really important for me to try to come to grips with was how there could possibly be men like the Europeans who massacred — how could you create that level of brutality in men and create horrible atrocities towards Indigenous peoples the world over?

And then I learned about the history of Europe — that as Christianity moved north, midwives, nurses, and so-called "witches" were sought after in a campaign of genocide — about four million women were killed by European leaders. So the reason that European men could do this to our people is because they had already cut the umbilical cord in their homeland.

I began to see the reasons for the feminist movement as a healing for white women. As Indigenous peoples we never experienced our men doing to us what European men had done to European women. I have never identified myself as a feminist even though we are all strong for the rights of our people. Some traditional cultures might tend to divide up the roles and responsibilities, it may be like we see in our ceremonies with the different roles of men and women, but I strongly respect the different ways we exist in the created world.

JY: What do you think about feminism today?

AC: A lot of the movement work that was going on in the 70s has changed. One thing you have to recognize is that's why we call it a movement — it changes. There is also a necessity to look at the gains — and sometimes the tendency is to say we don't need that anymore. People can forget the importance of keeping vigilant and keeping movement principles alive and applied to a new reality.

I know that they have taken away the Women's Studies Collective at UCSC but it's something that is worth learning from. What we did was taken to the whole collective and it was exciting in terms of empowerment. It was rigorous — maybe some people think we slacked off but we didn't. It was a student representative program, meaning we gave credits for working in the community on your own terms. My first job was working in a women's shelter in San Jose run by women of colour and Indigenous women — who were also the clientele.

Feminist philosophy is a historical reality for European women — some women of colour and Indigenous women identify with feminism and are helping to redefine it with their own cultural values. I think the work you are doing, Jessica, is a great example of this, when you ask for instance what does reproductive justice mean for Indigenous women who aren't even allowed to keep their own children? Many times we have been victimized not only by stopping pregnancies from happening as a policy, but because of larger environmental practices and policies in our lands that prevent us from having healthy pregnancies now, like spraying with pesticides, toxic mining, etc. It affects everything.

I want to say that I don't think we need to reject feminism though — I think we need to redefine it, find common points and common ground and involve Indigenous peoples and other communities of colour. As long as there is mutual respect and all of our cultural and historic realities are brought into the mix, we can create cross-cultural human movements.

* * *

Jesscia Yee is a self-described "Two-Spirit multi-racial Indigenous hip hop feminist reproductive justice freedom fighter". She is the founder and Executive Director of the Native Youth Sexual Health Network — the only organization of its kind in North America that works within the full spectrum of sexual and reproductive health by and for Indigenous youth across the continent.

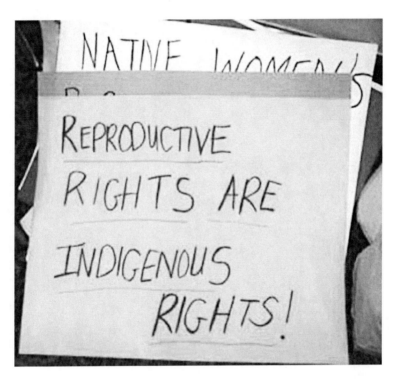

Sign created by Jessica Yee

BY KRYSTA WILLIAMS and ERIN KONSMO

Resistance to Indigenous Feminism

We decided to co-author this piece for a number of reasons. Considering the extremely persistent process of "dividing and conquering" our Indigenous communities, and especially our women to prevent collective action, it's pretty amazing when young Native women get together and talk about this stuff, let alone write about it! We met as Indigenous sisters, survived struggle together, and are united in our work going forward. We also both do amazing work on preventing HIV and supporting Aboriginal people living with HIV/AIDS, promoting sexual health by and for Native youth, understanding human rights as Indigenous Peoples, and advocating for sex worker rights — all with the Native Youth Sexual Health Network!

We had a lot of conversations about the fucked up resistance we have faced in expressing our awesome Indigenous Feminist views, ideas, perspectives and bodies in general. But we also had a lot of difficulty characterizing them into a couple of nouns and verbs that could be easily understood. So instead of battling it out to decide which working title we would use for our submission we thought it would be interesting to include them all!

- Young Native Women Ragin' it up with Feminism
- Taking back our Power: Young Indigenous Feminists enRAGEd
- Resistance to Indigenous Feminism
- Why we have a love/hate relationship with feminism
- Saying the "F" word: why being an Indigenous woman isn't enough (this title speaks to the fact that for us, being Indigenous will always come first, and we are the first real feminists, which is explained further in this piece)
- Isn't Indigenous & Feminist repetitive?
- How "Feminism" is still white and still colonial
- Has feminism been whitewashed?
- Get over it and be my sister: How "women's unity" is colonial
- Why I don't want to hold hands with you
- Fuck the 3 waves — We are the Ocean!
- Indigenous ~~Feminist~~ ? !INDIGENOUS!

Does the title "Resistance to Indigenous Feminism" mean the resistance we face from others as Indigenous feminists? Or does this speak to our internal resistance to the fact that we are forced to identify as feminists in this fucked up political women's movement?

It's BOTH!

This is our rationale for submitting a piece to a book about *Deconstructing the Academic Industrial Complex of Feminism*:

- **Deconstruction:** a word that speaks to breaking down. a reclamation of what is inherently and historically ours.

- **Academic:** the institutionalized, the inherently patriarchal and colonial. Claiming our spot as !INDIGENOUS! and what that means as !INDIGENOUS! women.

Reflections on Indigeneity and gender

Krysta: I was raised by my mother and grandmother primarily, and always resented Dr. Phil (a white American talk show host) when he proclaimed I would be "troubled" without a father, a man to tell me what to do. My mother was my father figure too. I had many uncles that to this day show me that "being a man" isn't all about drinking beer and John Deere. The fact that I had no awareness about the traditional teachings of Two-Spirit and Trans people (though they were no doubt part of my community) speaks to my own experiences with the erasure of Indigenous knowledge. I now have the privilege and honour of calling many Two-Spirit and Trans people friends and family from whom I learn and grow with.

Erin: Growing up I always had a struggle between hearing my mother speak and teach all of my siblings that gender was much less binary than what is so extreme in Alberta versus what my father sometimes showed me that I was up against. I believe that if the Traditional Knowledge of gender had been something I had known earlier then I could have at least understood and dealt with this struggle more easily. For example, at the Native Youth Sexual Health Network (NYSHN) our work is guided with the Indigenous understanding that there are ancestral roles of Two-Spirit leaders being medicine people, healers, and warriors. NYSHN works by many principles that are Two-Spirited. The Two-Spirit and Trans people in my life are amazing Indigenous Feminists, and a crucial piece to all of the discussions that follow.

We bet there are lots of amazing pieces in this collection about Indigenous concepts of gender and the awesome-ness that is our Two-Spirit community members. Read them.

Below is a dialogue between Indigeno'Us'. We choose to have a conversation in spirit of deconstructing academia and challenging the forms in which knowledge is accepted.

K: So, Erin we were having trouble coming up with a title for this article. Why do you think that is?

E: Well, I would have to say that feminism itself seems so out of touch that claiming a title was immensely hard and seemed almost ridiculous. Why the hell do I need to name what my struggle is?

K: Indeed! The idea that we need to be "understood" by "other" people in order to justify our thoughts and struggles is pretty fucked. I also find English extremely hard to work in, to express my thoughts or feelings about anything of substance is really tough. Then it makes me feel sad that I don't know my own language.

E: If I could describe what my struggles have been, continue to be, or talk about my mom, and grandmother it would likely include less words and perhaps be just the intimate interaction of an embrace. If our title could literally embody a hug this whole article would be a sweet loving embrace of the powerful women in our lives. How about that for a title?

K: Awww! As much as my first instinct is to call that "cheesy", I think it's pretty radical to express love and compassion when we are expected to be passive and stoic Indians. And I also think that feminism sets this bar of "independent, strong women" that are supposed to be able to "handle our emotions". But the Elders I know tell me that laughter and tears are medicine.

E: I definitely believe that since my mother and grandmother felt they could not cry, my body has taken that blood memory on and told me to embrace and reclaim those tears, to let them tell stories, and to use them to create new and beautiful relationships. *Tear*

K: Fuck yeah! I've learned so much about how to cry and how to laugh and how to be angry. Not violent, but express anger as an emotional reaction, and know that there is nothing wrong with that. My thoughts, opinions and conjectures are just as important and relevant as my feelings! And I want to deconstruct these ideas about "strength" and "weakness" that feminism has created.

E: These ideas of strength and independence have also created divides for our mothers and grandmothers and acted as yet another way to separate ourselves from the strength in our communities. That's why this academic, pushed-on us feminist shit has actually hurt my family!

K: I don't even know what "independent" means anymore. I think for a lot of folks it's impossible to not be dependent on someone (a partner, family member) or something, financially or otherwise in order to survive. This especially doesn't speak to our communities, where people depend on each other and share a lot for survival! We understand that things are connected and interdependent and this does NOT mean weakness.

E: So, I think this speaks to why we feel so strongly about "Taking back our Power: Young Indigenous Feminists enRAGEd". Are you enraged Krysta?

K: Do you have to ask?? Seriously though, the stereotype of "angry Native activist" can really silence my legitimate rage and anger at a system that has oppressed for so long. And this idea that people of colour are "loud" and "angry" is dismissive and undermines our experiences. I have a right to be angry! And in love! And hurt! And all sorts of feelings!

E: Girl, I gotta say that this reminds me of the rage that I felt but never understood as a youth growing up in rural Alberta. Sorry but I gotta break out my favorite Social Distortion song, "I Wasn't Born to Follow":

> When I grow up, gonna be a star
> Gonna sing my songs and play my guitar, I'm ready
> Gonna change the world, gonna turn the page
> Gonna say what I feel, let out this rage, get ready
> We're going down, down to the streets below
> I said "goodbye to the masses, I wasn't born to follow"

K: Sounds like you were ready to "deconstruct" the whole world! And it needs it.

E: I didn't understand a lot of the feelings that I had at this time in my life, but felt that I had rage that needed to be let out. That's been recognized in many ways as accepting that "I Wasn't Born to Follow" but ready to be on the streets and do the work that we are doing now. Some of these thoughts may seem disconnected, but these are the frustrations we have around talking about feminism and our experiences as Native women. We challenge you to not get defensive, but consider these random thoughts and ideas as our process of decolonization. Cultural appropriation is inherent to the "third wave" of feminism and the feminist unification project* — and that is just another form of neo-colonialism. As Indigenous peoples we feel it is important to recognize what is happening in this context of feminism in order to resist new forms of colonization, reclaim and write back as a part of the larger decolonization process. The third wave of feminism, in their attempt to be more "progressive" and erase the problematic history of feminism, tacks on Indigenous women to their list of "struggles we support" to try and differentiate from the first or second wave. In reality this is just a new way of colonizing us; taking credit for who we are, and not recognizing that they need to deal with their shit and allow us to be separate.

Note: "feminist unification project" are the words we use to describe the mentality of mainstream feminists needing to hold hands, learn from each other and be sisters, in one unified circle of feminism, in order to win the fight against patriarchy. But this denies our sovereignty as distinct Indigenous nations, each with our own language, culture, history and experience of colonization. It also assumes non-Indigenous people are a homogenous (same) group and denies the intersections of oppression, power and privilege.

First off, as has been well stated by many Indigenous Feminists before us, the idea of gender equality did not come from the suffragettes or other so-called "foremothers" of feminist theory. It should also be recognized that although we are still struggling for this thing called "gender equality", it is not actually a framed issue within the feminist realm, but a continuation of the larger tackling of colonialism. So this idea in mainstream feminism that women of colour all of a sudden realized "we are women", and magically joined the feminist fight actually re-colonizes people for who gender equality and other "feminist" notions is a remembered history and current reality since before Columbus. The mainstream feminist movement is supposed to have started in the early 1900s with women fighting for the right to vote. However, these white women deliberately excluded the struggles of working class women of colour and participated in the policy of forced sterilization for Aboriginal women and women with disabilities. Furthermore, the idea that we all need to subscribe to the same theoretical understandings of history is marginalizing. We all have our own truths and histories to live. We have the need to differentiate ourselves by race and politics because of historical injustices. Similarly we must differentiate our values as Indigenous Feminists lest we become the "default white women". White men are the default for society and positions of power; we also need to reset the false default settings for feminism (currently as white female suffragettes) to Indigenous Peoples who are the true origins of gender equality!

Thoughts about labelling and the personal vs. political from an Indigenous Feminist perspective

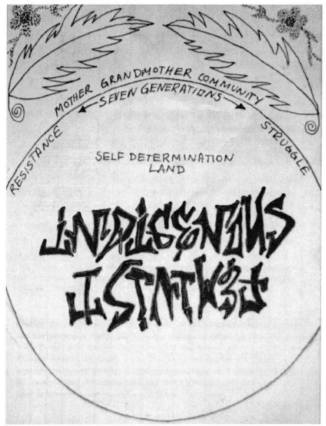

Image 1: Mirrored Images of Indigenous Peoples. By Erin Konsmo.

At the end of the day, we as Indigenous Feminists shouldn't have to wear a label in order to live our values. But we really do feel as though we do have to label until these concepts are understood and accepted as Indigenous Traditional Knowledge without question. All that the mainstream feminist movement is trying to claim today is merely a reflection of what an Indigenous person (including women, men, Two-Spirit, trans or different gender identifying people) sees when they look in the mirror (see Image 1). There is this feeling amongst "innovative thinkers" that we need to reach forward to build and/or discover a "new society" that includes gender equality. But we know that for us, as a community, this simply means a return to our Indigenous ways of life, a decolonization of our communities which will bring back gender equality. This is something that we have been fighting for and resisting since contact. However, being pushed forward by progressives while trying to hold onto and remember the past, honour our Elders and teachings — while being present — is a painful experience!

There is nothing more frustrating than other communities attaching themselves to this process of decolonization and saying "I like the idea of Two-Spirit people and wish I had that in my community". Although we encourage all communities to work issues specific to their realities, we are conscious of this process not being through the appropriation of the decolonization that is specific to our struggle as Indigenous Peoples. We are simultaneously trying to embrace the positive change that is happening in our hearts and homes, while still protecting our knowledge, our people and our communities from the violence that is appropriation. Please, if you're looking for stories of strength about women don't ask us for the creation stories specific to Indigenous people so that you can act it out in your performance.

Deconstructing the idea that "the personal is political"

Although we actively live struggles and have to be political, we also know that our struggles go far beyond just being personal and are tied to our communities, our land, and our ancestors. This is the Indigenous "personal is political". We do this work for the healing of our mothers, grandmothers and communities. It means taking it back for the last seven generations, some of whom weren't able to speak these words, and doing it for the next seven generations.

Fuck the "waves" of feminism: we embody over 500 years of resistance before us, and are working several generations ahead. We're an ocean.

So much of our struggle has been reduced to asking "who"? (Belongs to our community? Are we talking about? Fighting against?). We get distracted thinking about who and how we really are as Indigenous people which distracts and prevents us from tackling real issues of gender violence, of racism and ongoing colonization. At the same time, there needs to be space for these confusing discussions. We both spent a lot of time searching for someone or something to accept us as Indigenous people (the Indian Act and having "status cards" to "prove" your Indigeneity make this especially confusing). This caused us to hesitate in getting involved with community efforts to create positive change.

E: My great Auntie Bunny lived a personal struggle with structural racism that made it impossible for her to have safe access to reproductive health services like abortion while she was working as a sex worker. I also know that this structural racism was related to the raping of land that happened and continues to happen within the province of Alberta with the Tar Sands which breeds patriarchy and violence towards Aboriginal women. Her struggle while personal was also connected to years of our peoples land claim fights, intergenerational abuse, and environmental justice. Struggles while fought at an individual level are often a community struggle.

K: When I was first 'coming home'*, I struggled a lot with this. I felt like I didn't know who I was, disconnected from any sort of community. It took many Elders and friends to remind me to simply remember who I was, and do the work to get reconnected; put myself out there, contact family I had never met and just spend time with them. I had to learn about humility, to not focus so much on who I was but what I could do for my community.

Note: My understanding is that coming home refers to the process of reconnecting with family and community. I grew up in a very loving family, but I did not know all my relations until later in my youth. Meeting my Grandmother for the first time in the summer of 2008 was extremely inspiring!

The struggle between individual liberation vs. self-determination for our communities and healing

What does it mean for an individual to be considered "liberated"? What does it mean for Indigenous communities to be "liberated"? I think the pictures we think of as Native women are very different than the end goals that are expressed in a lot of feminist literature. In other words, there needs to be more space given to community-based solutions and the hard work that everyone, especially women in our communities do every day.

In academia (and in general) we are still struggling with tokenism. Including one article or person of colour, or Indigenous person into feminist curriculum is not enough. This needs to be fully integrated into all women's studies curriculum (which is still inherently racist).

E: One crucial element that non-Indigenous academia needs to accept is that no matter how much you read the journals of Columbus, a Native chief, or through interviews of Native people you do not have the blood memory that we have within us. Sorry, if this ruins your PhD on Native people but you don't have the blood memory experiences that I do and so the internal "validity" of your research will never compare!

K: Internal validity has never been so literal...It also needs to be understood that including folks after the fact just doesn't cut it. White supremacy exists within institutions and this can't be changed by just putting Indigenous bodies into chairs. There are structural changes that we have been calling for since forever!

Labelling is no longer a liberating political act but a necessity in order to gain entrance into the academic industrial complex and other discussions and spaces. For example, if so called "radical" or "progressive" people don't hear enough "buzz" words (like feminist, anti-oppression, anti-racist, social justice, etc.) in your introduction, then you are deemed unworthy and not knowledgeable enough to speak with authority on issues that you have lived experience with. The criteria for identifying as a feminist by academic institutions, peer reviewed journals, national bodies, conferences, and other knowledge gatekeepers is very exclusive. It is based on academic theory instead of based on lived experiences or values. Name-dropping is so elitist! You're not a "real" feminist unless you can quote, or have read the following white women: (insert Women's Studies 101 readings).

It is interesting that we feel we need to write this to white feminists. I also want to call out to all my sisters who are grappling with this "feminist stuff", unsure of what to call ourselves. We are the embodiment of the fight for self-determination! This is NOT a theoretical discussion, these are our lives!

Because this is our life we decided to write a bit about, **give credit to and acknowledge all the women in our lives who have taught us everything we know about feminism, without ever labelling themselves** as such. We dedicate this piece to them, since they taught us pretty much everything we know. Here goes!

Krysta's ancestor piece

The following is a piece I (Krysta) wrote about one of the many Indigenous Feminists in my life, who taught me about it meant to be a strong Native woman. However, she does not identify as a feminist for many reasons and I wouldn't have it any other way.

> She is my sister, my mother, my Auntie and my friend. She is traditional and radical. The most hilarious and grounded person I know. Despite her chronic pain and oppression she's there for me.

> She is a gifted singer and a carrier of the drum, a lodge conductor and a mother. She helps women find their voice, and not just for singing. She even helped me find my voice, and my family. When I doubt myself she tells me lovingly to remember who I am and where I come from.

> People tease her because she is very strict with her ceremonial protocol. "Oh Christine, and her rules!", they say. But I have learned a neverendingrespect for doing ceremony the same way my ancestors have done it for thousands of years — while still making it my own.

I can only hope that I am brave enough to live up to the teachings she so freely shares, in the hope of building strong women with strong voices. Her heart is steady and my hope is strong.

She can be gentle and she can be fierce. She is loud yet we so easily forget her words when they are not what we want to hear. She has been mistreated, abused, celebrated and revered. To me, her shoulders must be so broad and strong to bear this burden of history.

She taught me to eat the green part of my strawberry. "It's medicine," she said. "At least put it outside if you won't eat it, we don't put medicine in the garbage." We would see women who found their voice, and then forgot their teachings of humility and respect. "You have to learn how to crawl like a worm, before you can soar like an eagle."

I like worms. And sea gulls. And crows. We all give reverence to eagles and hawks. But these animals are gifts from the Creator too with their own essential teachings. They are just as important and we can never forget that.

Kitchen Table Wisdom, we call it. Sharing stories of so-called "dysfunctional, alcoholic" families that we both have. But it's funny! We can find humour in just about anything — it's how we survive, thrive and adapt.

A Haudenosaunee, an Anishinaabe — an unlikely friendship. But I think we are, simply, a beautiful song.

Erin's ancestor piece

This piece contains two Indigenous women among many who have had a significant impact on the feminism that drives my spirit, that continuously informs that spirit and who were Indigenous Feminists in so many instinctive and natural ways. Indigenous ways.

My mother April and my Grandmother Marie have had a profound and nourishing impact on my life. They influence my character, spirit, perseverance, and continue to in ways that I will never understand. They are my living, breathing, spiritual, Indigenous Feminism. Many of the same characteristics come from my grandmother and mother. Both of them have always been very strong, enduring hardship yet maintaining their humour. A sense of responsibility was instilled among our family, driven by humility and a connection with allowing a larger community to also be a part of our hearts. No matter how hard times were, there was always enough food for an extra stranger or someone from the neighbourhood.

Speaking of food, how weird it was to grow up and find out that the doughgots* that I was eating were actually just bannock, covered up — like much of my history.

They both adamantly believed and taught me that a woman had strengths that built community, were leaders through vision, and that being a strong woman was at its peak when we were closest to the spirit world while raising children. The strongest aspect of Indigenous Feminism that was passed down to me came from my mother and grandmothers appreciation for their roles in mothering. My Grandma and mother both strongly believed in lifelong learning, taking risks and reaching out for opportunity and possibility. If you found yourself feeling safe then you weren't learning and growing.

I feel honoured to have been passed down the creativity they instilled in me through their love for art, beading, sewing, crafts, and gardening. They both taught me an appreciation for every living part of my environment and to care for my surroundings. My grandmother knew every herb, every mushroom, flower, grass, berry, and bird. This connection keeps my hands focused and busy, while maintaining my wonder and connection with environment.

Two of the most fundamental teachings that came from these women for me were:

Adversity builds character. After a storm, things will stand on more solid ground than they did before. And to always send forward compassion in my life.

Note: My mom called bannock "doughgots" because if you ate too much fried dough then you got a 'gut' ache. So, adding dough+gut made doughgots.

* * *

Krysta Williams *is an Indigenous Feminist and Turtle clan from Moravian of the Thames First Nation. She is a traditional singer and drummer, learning songs and teachings from the many amazing women in Kitchener-Waterloo, Ontario. Krysta is the Lead Youth Advocate at the Native Youth Sexual Health Network, with a degree in Psychology and Spanish and Latin American Studies from the University of Waterloo. She is currently on the board of directors for the Waterloo Public Interest Research Group (WPIRG) — a social and environmental justice organization for and by students and community members. She is passionate about food justice, Indigenous self-determination and healing our relationship with the land.*

Erin Konsmo *is a Cree, Norwegian Indigenous feminist/artist from Innisfail, Alberta. She is the Alberta representative on the National Aboriginal Youth Council on HIV/AIDS and an Intern for the Native Youth Sexual Health Network. She is currently taking her Master's of Environmental Studies at York University.*

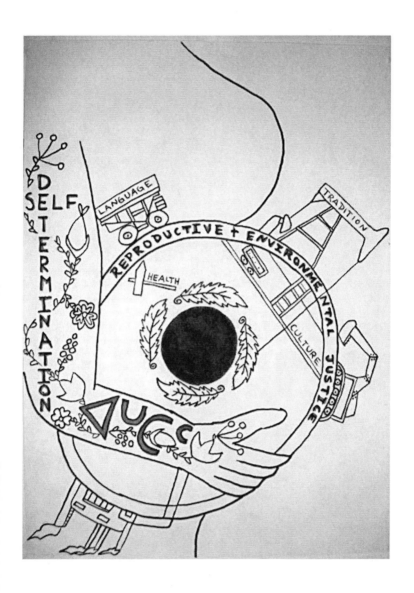

ReproEnviroJustice by Erin Konsmo

A Slam on Feminism in Academia

BY SHAUNGA TAGORE

why did you let me through the doors in the first place
if you were just gonna turn around and force me out?

why did you let me in this ivory tower
filled with hippie feel-good activist academics
debating about feminist organizing in high theory discourse
while barely-paid migrant workers prepare lunches
for seminars, conferences, forums
and get deported the next day

an award winning tenured professor once told me
the only way i will succeed at graduate school
is if i read 300 pages of theory per week per class
and if i'm not capable
my writing must be of low quality
my intellect must be incredibly juvenile

nothing could be wrong with the way things are
because to change the rules would
undermine what it means to receive a graduate school education
and would leave me unprepared to
compete for future jobs and faculty positions

let me ask you
exactly which graduate student's education are you concerned about
here?

not single mothers who need extra time to look after their families
not pregnant women who need a little more maternity leave

not low-income folks who need to take 2nd or 3rd jobs
to pay bills their funding doesn't cover
not racialized international students who don't have access to most
scholarships

not the people with disabilities
who don't have access to comply with the way things are
made to feel something is wrong with them
instead of with the rules themselves

not those who survive sexual violence
and need extra time to grieve rage or deal

not anyone with familial, historical ties
to places and races always under siege
living under governments set on killing their people

who must spend free time at sit-ins or rallies
where emotions and exhaustions run too high
drumbeats and chants ring too loud
to read a detached article due for class the next day

not Indigenous students who are expected
to read speak and engage with
languages, theories, and knowledges
that erase appropriate and colonize
their lands, cultures, and selves
with the same ease as the colonizers

not people of colour subjected to
subtle and blatant racism
making it impossible to participate
the same way as their white peers

not anyone who needs to spend every moment of their leisure time
finding other ways of learning
through art, community activism, collective therapy
(or a mashup of all three)

your ideal graduate student is
someone who doesn't have to experience community organizing
because you've already assigned them five chapters to read about it

your ideal graduate student is
someone who can't talk about positionality or privilege
without referencing some article

your ideal graduate student is
rich enough
white enough
straight enough
able-bodied and -minded enough
to be given luxury of enjoying sitting in a corner reading 900 pages a
week
(with their fair trade starbucks coffee in hand and their lulu lemon track
pants on ass)

your ideal graduate student
IS NOT ME

so WHY did you let me through these doors in the first place
if you were just gonna turn around and shove me out?

to fill some quota for affirmative action?
to appear like a progressive program without putting in the effort
of actually being one?

don't pretend you're not secretly wishing you could
impersonate my lawyer to kidnap me
and deport me in a heartbeat
if i did so much as look at you funny
talk back
write an angry poem
and undermine your authority

by rolling my eyes at your hypocrisy

feminism in academia – OWN UP TO YOURSELF
do not pretend to be the godsend intellectually paving the revolution

recognize that the ones let through these doors by some strategic mis-
take
are the ones making you look good
while we burn out and burn up by your hands

what is it about your knowledge and education
that prevents you from imagining
all the different reasons someone may be in graduate school
or feel the need to study gender, race, sexuality, and class?

some of us are not here to one day
soullessly recite the entire cannon of queer theory development
with our hearts and minds closed

some of us do not wish to compete to be the
newest biggest baddest radical faculty-hire

some of us need to engage with feminist theory
so we can ground it in our community activist work
our creative works
our personal relationships
for our families, communities and histories
for our own fucking deserved peace of minds

maybe we need to know how to make sense of oppression
because we're so heartbroken

we don't want to end up being locked away in psychiatric institutions
or in a hospital overdosed on pills, getting our stomachs pumped
because we don't know WHY all this shit is constantly driving us CRAZY

what i want to know is why the fuck YOU were let through these doors
and made to think you could decide all the rules FOR US?

you tell me my intellect is lacking

i'm not worthy of being here
if i'm not capable of doing exactly what you say
exactly your way

but i choose to follow the kind of wisdom your 300 pages per week per class
could never teach you

it's gotten me this fucking far

* * *

Shaunga Tagore *is a writer, artist and arts-educator who lives in Toronto. She currently coordinates Asian Arts Freedom School, a radical Asian history and arts program, is an editor for* Shameless Magazine, *and is working on putting out her first collection of poetry called "The Erasable Woman." Keep in touch by visiting her website: www.shaungatagore.com.*

LATOYA PETERSON

The Feminist Existential Crisis (Dark Child Remix)

(If) I think (about gender, access, and equality), therefore I am (by definition, a feminist).

It should all be so simple, right? But in the immortal words of Lauryn Hill in "Ex-Factor:"

> but you had to make it hard/loving you is like a battle/and we both end up with scars
> tell me who I have to be/to get some reciprocity

To accept an identity as a "professional" feminist is to accept the layers of baggage associated with the label feminist. Added to the class and race parcels I carry, I find myself changing into Erykah Badu's metaphorical bag lady — even while I'm trying to let it go and let love heal some of these wounds. If I make my living unpacking racism and sexism, why willingly take on more?

But one thing is clear — the culture of professional feminism is crowding my space.

I never set out to become a professional feminist. I never really thought about becoming a feminist at all. Instead, I was just a precocious kid who loved to read, and I roamed the stacks at my neighborhood library the way some kids browse racks at clothing stores. Hanging out in my favorite section (the low 300s, where the old Dewey Decimal system shelved sociology and culture books), I stumbled across a the work that would start me on my journey.

Standing out from the shelf was a dark red, well-worn paperback boasting the title of *Manifesta: Young Women, Feminism, and the Future*. I pulled it off the shelf, spotted a reference to *Xena: Warrior Princess*, and checked it out that day, dodging lampposts as I read on the way home. As the years have gone by, I've mostly forgotten the content of the book itself - but I remember it made an impression on me, particularly as I relate to feminism primarily through pop culture. I was one of the pop-culture kids they talked about, the one who wondered why my male friends laughed at my Spice Girls inspired tees that read "Girl Power," the one who loved comics but preferred the sisterhood showed in the Japanese anime *Sailor Moon*, and who came of age in that era on the cusp: where Alanis Morissette and Britney Spears both reigned, when TLC and Little Kim where both holding it down. It was *Manifesta* that prompted me to ask the question "What is a feminist anyway?" and through my journey, many many books later, to answer that a feminist was what I was.

I read everything I could by and about women, looking for what was common in our narratives. Ever racially conscious, I soon decided to look outside of the established feminist canon for nourishment, knowing that black women and feminism had a rocky history between them. When I stumbled upon Joan Morgan's *When Chickenheads Come Home to Roost: A Hip Hop Feminist Breaks It Down*, I felt like I had finally found a home. I read. I wrote. I blogged. And somewhere along the way, people started acknowledging me as a feminist writer. And then just a feminist. And then inviting me to speak at women-focused events and feminist conferences.

Somehow, that became my identity for a while. Yet, underneath my skin, I was always chafing. I felt like I was constantly explaining class and race in relation to feminism, even with those who didn't want to hear it. I started seeing the same hierarchies play out time and time again. I stopped feeling so connected to the women and girls I wanted to speak to, and started to feel like I was being pulled into a very different world.

Now, it's always a different world than where you come from. But this was way different. It was wealthier, whiter, full of events and fetes and conferences. It was earnest. It was aware. But not too aware, since I always felt like I wore the cloak of the outsider. I've made a lot of wonderful friends through feminism, and got to meet so many more amazing women, and yet I always had this feeling that I still hadn't quite landed where I was supposed to be. It was as if I was on this path, but it was leading away from where I was trying to go. Somehow, I always ended up feeling isolated.

This became clear when *More Magazine* asked if I wanted to be one of their featured young feminists. A friend reached out to me to encourage me to do it, specifically noting "yeah, there aren't a lot of women of colour being represented." So I signed up and contacted the reporter. Despite loving the amazing women I met, and feeling thankful to *More* for the exposure, I felt like I couldn't breathe in that space. It was as if everything I had been thinking and feeling about feminism bubbled to the forefront of my mind. While everyone else chatted and chatted about book deals and the trials involved in being a modern feminist, my mind kept drifting away from the event. Why was I here? Did I even want to do this work anymore? I got into feminism because I wanted to talk to young girls like me. Girls that grew up in the same way as my friends and I did. Girls that were facing those same hard decisions.

Instead, I was finding myself giving talks to groups of earnest young college-educated white girls, being interviewed, having endless conversations about why I needed an agent, why I needed a book deal, why I need to know XXX professional feminist. I felt like I was stuck doing a slow boxstep when I really wanted to samba.

Since I was bound and restricted emotionally, being forced to freeze smiles on my face and pose in one place to model for our big feminist group shot was really was the only appropriate way to spend the afternoon.

I left there with my head in a bad place. How exactly did I get to this place, covered in make-up, at a warehouse in New York, feeling at the top of my game but also alienated from everything. I started out just wanting to talk (or, er, type — blogging is my medium). So I did. I talked about race and gender. I talked about rape and not rape and all the things in between. I wrote about

45

music videos and socialization. I wrote about rap lyrics and my feminist awakening. I devoured Joan Morgan and Gwendolyn D. Pough and Andreana Clay. But I kept ending up stuck. Defending who I was, time and time again. Feeling like I had tried to claim some space, but failed, ending up as a panel showpiece.

I started shying away from gatherings and discussions of feminism. The discomfort I wanted abate by declaring myself a feminist only became more complicated when I agreed to do more feminist things. For some reason, after more than three years talking about gender issues, I felt more alienated from the feminist movement than ever.

Could it be that I wasn't a feminist then? I kept thinking and thinking, but the definitive "I AM" seemed to get farther and farther away. A friend of mine expressed puzzlement when I floated the idea of giving up the label "feminist", asking if that meant I had given up my beliefs in gender equality. That wasn't the case at all — but I had started to feel significantly less invested in the endless, circular discussions about the proper way to practice feminism, the who's who list, the removal of my rough ideas on feminism from everyday life. Ultimately, I realized I didn't care enough to continue operating in that space. Feminism is part of the tool kit of my everyday life and a large part of my identity. But it wasn't the be all end all, and I ultimately wanted to devote that mental space somewhere else.

And so I did.

Then, one cold winter day, I got an email from an old icon: Jennifer Baumgardner. The author of *Manifesta*, the book I had picked up so long ago from the library and read at the very beginning of my feminist awakening was asking me to come and be on a panel in New York. I agreed, wondering what I would say, considering how I was on unstable ground with feminism anyway. I wondered a lot of things. Could I even read *Manifesta* now? I had changed, learned a different prism for looking at feminist issues — ultimately, I was afraid of being disappointed with something I had treasured growing up. It wouldn't have been the first time. Another one of the panelists was a very famous and very important writer who walked in with a swagger and laid down declarations, never pausing to consider the impact of preaching a one-true feminism to the malleable young minds in attendance.

Sitting on the panel, I realized there was nothing I could say that would make me satisfied. My crisis was full and total - what could I say to them that would affirm their feminism at a time when I was so deeply questioning my own.

So I told the only story I could tell convincingly: my own.

And I told the truth as I understood it.

And at this moment, at a crossroads in my journey, those two things will have to be enough.

* * *

When she isn't pondering the meaning of life, feminism, and every-thing (answer: 42), **Latoya Peterson** *can be found hanging out in DC or on her couch playing video games. She edits the blog* Racialicious *as a way to justify her pop culture consumption habits.*

LOUIS ESME CRUZ

Medicine Bundle of Contradictions
Female-man, Mi'kmaq/Acadian/ Irish Diasporas, Invisible disAbilities, masculine-Feminist

English is neither of my Mother-tongues, nor is it the language of my Father. Neither is the land upon which I type this out, from Anishinaabekwe/Three Fires Territory. I hope this reaches you in ways useful and compassionate, as words that might assist you (and me) to comprehend the world of complexities we live in. Sometimes life confuses me and I've found that re-writing what I see and experience in life gives me the chance to respond to the indignities of life, creating beauty from chaos. This bundle of words is to "deconstruct the academic industrial complex of feminism" smudging this machine that attempts to re-colonize Indigenous gender roles.

What I experience through this empathic heart and tough flesh, in these sturdy bones wrapped in the tendons of memory, is not always visible in daily life. This body, a bundle of contradictions strung together to carry me between worlds, carrying knowledge, food, passion and stories — all as medicines to tend the complexities of life, with all my relations. My life is a continual cycle of learning/unlearning and loving/unloving. Like many people affected by invasion, I have learned to survive above living. Bringing myself back to life is a process, not a destination. When I'm surviving, it can feel as though simple things are out of reach, like enjoyment or pleasure. In these moments, I find it difficult to relax and grow from the sweat of my love/work. I write this to you, making something beautiful in this shared space between us, making it is difficult for invasion to take root here. When we recognize each other, it is easier for both of us to relax. We build what Lee Maracle, recognized Sto:lo author, describes as the golden rainbow between us. Maracle says that when we build this arch, we are actively resisting invasion because no two objects can occupy the same space at the same time.

One of the books I look to for guidance in helping me grow golden rainbows between the past and present, to undo how colonization has invaded my thoughts, is Mi'kmaq *Hieroglyphic Prayers*, a wicked book edited by Murdena Marshall and David Schmidt. In it, the authors heal an old relationship between Christian missionary, Chrestien LeClerc and the first identified Indigenous language in North America. Christianity invaded Mi'kmaq life/land and removed us from how we described ourselves, lived in our bodies and related to our home. This was how we knew ourselves. Now we know ourselves as something else because this is the way it is. LeClerc organized Mi'kmaq written language so he could replace our spiritual ways with his Christian ones. In *Morning Prayer*, LeClerc takes the Mi'kmaq word for shaman/mediciner/healer, *puo'in*, translates it and steals it from us. LeClerc pushed love away from the importance of *puo'in* to our families and our bodies, replacing it with hate. Here is where this happens:

> iknmul ntelue'wuti'l oqoj aqq msit koqoe'l winjikl tpuk pewayapn mntue'l puo'winue'l aqq msit koqoe'l winjikl masklteman ntinin.

> Let me hate all my sins and all the wicked things I dreamt of this morning, the things of the devil, of the shaman, and all evilness that is in my body.

This line has me asking: What are my sins — sleeping orgasms? What is wicked about all the things I dreamt of this morning — my friend's sexy dance moves? How is the devil the same thing as the shaman — because s/he has medicines that help me sleep and be awake through the trauma of invasion? What is evil in my body — how it feels when I watch my friend's sexy dance moves while taking medicines from the shaman? An even bigger question, perhaps the most important one is: What does God have to do with hating myself, my dreams, my medicine and my body?

This line feels gross in my flesh and bones. It is the thick sludge of self-hate. While I understand that nothing in the universe is without "positive" and "negative" forces, things are way off balance when humans are telling each other that *Kisulk* (Creator) wants us to hate who we are. What LeClerc did not anticipate is that while there would be many generations where gender relations would be imbalanced in our families, clans and nations — we have pulled through. We look different now, from our wide range of skin tones to the style of clothes we wear. We still know where we're from and who our families are. The balance comes in the form of acknowledging and accepting that things are different now, that this is okay and we can find words to describe ourselves in new and old ways. Two-Spirit people will always be Two-Spirit people. It is who we are. What the arrogance of invasion could not have known is the strength within us that is more complex than hate, gifted to us by *Kisulk*, which would see us through to the other side of violence. Whether LeClerc intended to be an invasive person I do not know, and it is not important anyway. It *is* important that we gently undo the effects of violence and follow through with this undoing.

Maliseet artist and herbalist, Shirley Bear, points out the actions/minds of the invaders in her poem, *History Resource Material*:

> Arrogant men in long black robes,
> baptizing and renaming...
> You should be
> Saved. You will be renamed!

Bear is telling us where to look for examples of this violence and gives us the opportunity to heal the parts of ourselves affected by this misnaming. She also mocks Catholicism's own "teachings" of not-taking-the-lord's-name-in-vain when she pleads, "For God's sake," in the poem's last line. Arrogance and renaming are creepy colonial friends, keeping power among male-men.

This is important for me to share with you when we are talking about unhinging the vice grip of feminism from Two-Spirit people's lives. I've noticed in many ways how white feminists think it's doing a good thing in spreading reproductive rights to "other" cultures that have also experienced European invasion, and like Native people of Turtle Island, are also dealing with the consequences. One of the ways I have experienced feminism re-settling (or re-invading) Turtle Island is

I am greatly uncomfortable with how I have seen settler feminists claim space and each others' bodies: it seems a lot like how land is manhandled as a resource that only some get to benefit from.

through "women-only" spaces. They claim that being a woman means being born female and that all who live as women and female are capital "F" feminists needing space without males and men.

"Women-only" spaces say that only people who experience misogyny and sexism are people born female and that this means being a woman. This is a gender binary that says that there are only two genders (man and woman), two sexes (male and female) and that they exist as opposites to each other. Women who were born biologically male are sometimes included in these spaces, though from what I've seen so far this doesn't happen very often; and Trans-women are asserting their dignity to be seen and treated as the women they are. I have also been invited into these spaces as a female-man before I medically transitioned and even now — if I disclose that I was born female and still have my ovaries and uterus. I need to say that I don't think there is anything offensive about people needing space to identify similar experiences, grow languages and relationships, and to celebrate life. I am greatly uncomfortable with how I have seen settler feminists claim space and each others' bodies: it seems a lot like how land is manhandled as a resource that only some get to benefit from.

It is a loving commitment to live in a way that does not oppress other people. All of the values we have inherited, whether from our parents or the Canadian over-culture, need to be looked at honestly. Once we look at these values we can decide which ones we are going to feed and which ones we will starve.

"Safety" is a value worth looking at. Being a "safe place" implies that harm will not happen while people are sharing that space. Popular sexual health education talks about how we can never be entirely safe from sexually transmitted infections while having sex, though we can reduce harm by using condoms, lube, communicating our limits, etc. If people cannot keep themselves "safe" during sex, it is usually because they — usually the person being penetrated or receiving — are in a position where someone else has the power. Therefore, safe sex is limited to the amount of choice the person being penetrated has over their surroundings. It is never appropriate to blame someone for not using a condom if they are the receptive sexual partner.

Similarly, Two-Spirit people are not allowed to participate in societies as our full selves and then we are shamed and blamed for the ways we are hurt by this. When people say that a space is "women-only" they are assuming that women are always sensitive to each others' needs, are always able to understand each others' experiences, these experiences are always the same and women are not violent. Explicity, this says that all women are safe; all men are unsafe. The inclusion of Two-Spirit people in women-only space is arbitrary, shifting with who has the power to define this space. This person in power is rarely Native. From what I have seen, women who parade feminist ideals are the ones who decide who experiences gender oppression. Two-Spirit people can talk about our oppression only when it parallels women's experiences. When our lives get too complicated we are judged, ignored, punished, humiliated. Whether it's women-only or men-only space, the naming of a space as only one gender encourages invasion and conquest because they don't allow people to be the complex creatures we are. This pushes Two-Spirit people to the margins simply because we are not one thing or another. We need liberation from the confines of gender baggage, too. This parallels the larger call from Indigenous sovereignty movements asking for our Native Nations to be recognized as distinct, sovereign entities. We are necessarily unique and complex for a reason.

These thoughts of separateness affect the minds of Two-Spirit people in profound ways. I've found myself in circumstances where we are policing each other's genders just like how we ourselves are treated by Christianity and colonial Canada. This started with Christian missionaries like Chrestian LeClerc and carries on today in how our families act like we are somehow not an essential part of them. As a way to heal this, I'm thinking about how Maracle describes what's between us as a golden rainbow where we can grow understanding. I know it is not as momentarily satisfying as holding a rally at city hall, but taking the time to get to know each other, gently, is one way that we can build that golden rainbow between us. This is trust building.

Two-Spirit people are as diverse as the lands we come from and the languages that describe our unique role/abilities. If you are interested in the origin of this term, I suggest reading Gregory Scofield (Metis Cree) or Qwo-Li Driskill (Cherokee) as they have done some great work that talks about these issues of language, nation, land and her/histories. A few things Two-Spirit people from all Native Nations have in common are that we can embody, literally, masculinity and femininity roles with strength; we can play with our genders, sexes and sexualities to point out how serious all of us can be; we're sexy, hot and fierce; and, unfortunately, we have had our experiences appropriated, misunderstood, categorized, diagnosed, institutionalized, neglected and hated simple because we exist. The things that bind us are not separate from each other. Of course we have always been fabulous, but we've become ultra-fierce since having to deal with being hated by our families and living in cities with our new families.

English is a very limited language that doesn't give very many options for explaining gender expressions and roles. Indigenous languages, like Mi'kmaq, focus on verbs (actions) rather than nouns (people, places or things), so the gender of a person is not as important as their actions.

English is a very limited language that doesn't give very many options for explaining gender expressions and roles. Indigenous languages, like Mi'kmaq, focus on verbs (actions) rather than nouns (people, places or things), so the gender of a person is not as important as their actions. In English, the language of invasion, nouns are emphasized. Invasion gives special privileges to people who haven't earned it — it is ill-logical. I notice how the work of trans people, women and Two-Spirit people are undervalued. What is considered "work" by the dominant culture of colonial Canada doesn't really fly for many of us, especially if we aren't recognized as the gender(s) we know ourselves to be because society has strict ideas about what makes a man a man, and a woman a woman. Because of this, we create work by our own definition, even though this may not pay all the bills, or falls outside the arbitrary laws of colonial Canada, or reinforces a relationship of dependence on this system, or puts extra stress on our lives. Whether our work is illegal or legit, we are often paid less than our settler co-workers or peers, given fewer opportunities for raises and promotions, scrutinized for no reason, expected to educate people who have higher wages than us about an assumed, singular Native way, are not supposed to expect more from life than what we are given, are kept in our place through use of force, criticism or ignorance. Two-Spirit people experience racism, miscegenaphobia, homophobia, transphobia, sexism, classism, fatphobia, and ableism — just like other people do — but add to that the fact that we are treated as if we are the problem because we can't or don't want to fit in with settler societies, including the feminist academic industrial complex.

Gender is not a culture, it is a role within culture.

Gender is not a culture, it is a role within culture. It can be difficult for us to remember, as Two-Spirit people, that we are sacred and to treat each other with sacredity with our complex lives inside and outside ourselves. I want for us to have the space to be all the beautiful things we are because this simple act of being ourselves defies invasion in two ways: by refusing to be erased as a Indigenous Peoples and refusing erasure as multigendered, sexual people. Our ability to be both these things and move between distinct yet connected worlds is our medicine. Whether these roles are human-made or given to us by *Kisulk*, I do not know enough to say, as I only know my own way, though I have a feeling that it is both. I am who I am and this is not just an identity or a set of beliefs. I am, literally, a continuation of my ancestors who resisted invasion in whatever ways they could to get me here.

Sanctuary, rather than safety, gives us places to rest and gather our internal resources to go back out again to a world needing radical transformation, at best. I thoroughly enjoy time with my

Two-Spirit family for these reasons, though I need this space to be open to anyone who needs to be there, regardless of appearance or identity. Undoing invasion in my own life has called me to question how appearance and identity are tricksters, *ki'kwaju* (wolverine), the illusion of safety. *Ki'kwaju* plays with my expectations, desires and assumptions. Always this trick is on me.

Sanctuary asks me to look into the heart/behaviours of people while simultaneously addressing the relationship of her/histories to the present moment. This bundle of complexity is medicine in a world bent on spiritual destruction through material obsession. Invaders go around forcibly renaming things and bundling up our relatives (trees, grasses, rocks, plants, fish, crustaceans, mammals, insects, minerals and more) to sell off for full profit, while keeping us busy arguing over blood quantum, morality, "tradition", band offices and shopping malls. It is easy in this new way of doing things to forget to look after each other and ourselves, to provide sanctuary with our bodies and spirits in the midst of this colonial havoc. We get distracted by *ki'kwaju* who keeps us tangled in cycles of coping with invasion rather than using our humungous creative forces to transform landscapes, inside and out.

Respected and recently passed Mohawk thinker, Patricia Monture, shared in her writing how feminism is an innately Indigenous philosophy, intricately connected to her Mohawkness (my interpretation). My own Mother recently shared with me how her feminist friends chided her for not using birth control when she could have, and instead having six children and being a housewife. She laughs when she tells me this now, as we discuss how she only ever wanted to be a Mother and how she did work from home, using her creative and bartering skills to make ends meet. There is no feminist theory that could make me feel more loved than knowing how my Mother's work cared for our family.

What we also talk about, my Mama and I, is how obnoxious men can be when they do not know who they are or their responsibilities. Over 10 years ago when I told my Mother I wanted to medically transition and live as a man, one of her many responses was simply, "Are you sure? Do you know what men are like?" We laugh about this now, how in my stubbornness I took this to mean that she was unsupportive of my decision. Really, she was calling out the indignities men have created, expressing her fear of how men use their roles in family and culture without looking at the whole picture.

I haven't ever taken it lightly, these indignities. Being a female-man is simply who I am. Accessing hormones and surgery have helped me in ways to be grounded in shifting sanctuaries, affording me the space to carve out more space for others. Being a Two-Spirit man is my role and holding space for others to come undone, putting themselves back together again in their own ways, is part of my responsibilities. I take it seriously and am learning to laugh at how serious I can be with this. Whenever possible, I redirect the gaze that unquestioningly falls on my masculine-looking, light-skinned self by the dominant culture back to the place it needs residence: Two-Spirit people and women who take responsibility for themselves and all people, all-too-often ignored and disrespected.

Here is some of the knowledge of my body, my experience: My family is from at least three distinct places I know of: Springfield, New Brunswick; Swords, Co. Dublin, Ireland; Southern France. I have dark hair with flecks of gold, red and white; my skin is a pale olive tone though my cheeks flush red easily; my eyes are sparkle hazel. I am built sturdy, thick, furry and tall-ish. Amoung my blood relatives, I am the "dark one" who is "not fat, just big-boned". My chest is flat through the use of surgical enhancement. Like my Aunt Mona, I have been able to grow a beard since puberty, though as an adult I have decided to use synthetic androgenic hormones to enhance my "secondary-male sex traits" and am thoroughly covered in dark hair. My Mama birthed my female body 32 years ago when she was 32, and has supported me to live my adult life as a man. I can be sharp-tongued and sticky sweet and ambivalent. I do not yet fluently speak or write Mi'kmaq, nor Gaelic, nor Acadian French. I was raised in the Roman Catholic tradition — the religion of a single male prophet who appropriated our heroines and dubbed them saints. My parents encouraged us kids to question the Church but we were still required to attend weekly mass. We went where the work was, if there was any, so my younger sister and I grew up on Coast Salish, Cree and Blackfoot territories while my older siblings remember Mi'kmaqiq and Haudenosaunee territories as home. I have yet to visit our homes and families in Springfield, New Brunswick; Swords, Co. Dublin, Ireland; Southern France. I feel most at home by the water and mountains. I was raised on Welfare cheques, food bank lines, debt-management and sex trade. I went to state-funded Catholic public schools in "Alberta", then state-funded secular public schools in the "Fraser Valley" of "British Columbia". I ran away from home when I was 18 to work in the youth-driven, non-profit job market, restaurant/food service sectors, the Arts/Academia and barely survived off disability welfare. My body appears able and my mind clear, though I live with chronic pain and brain fog. My scars are, for the most part, invisible. I graduated from Emily Carr University with a BFA, the second in my immediate and extended family on Turtle Island to obtain a degree. It was one of the best things I have ever done for my self-esteem. My Mom is proud to call me her son and this means everything to me. Telling you these things are liberating.

Two pieces of information helped me move away from my family of origin and find sanctuary in an urban, multi-racial community: my older sister returning with gay dance music after her first year at university; the other, my Mom's friend sharing feminist principles with me about choice and agency. Both these women showed me another way where Two-Spirit people and women love and struggle with each other to make something new. The music of the gay pop band, Erasure, ironically taught me that men have high voices and make beautiful things. My Mom's feminist friend taught me that though life is difficult, I must never let myself be victimized. Shirley Bear writes, "I think Aboriginal people in this generation are changing the ideas of the world." I think she is right. Gay music and feminist thought helped me escape from home, but it is Native youth who brought me back with dignity, love and honesty. I am not white and I am not red. I am both. I am not gay and I am not straight. I am both. I am not a woman and I am not a man — you get the idea. I am unique.

I think that because I am able to balance my selves, I can give love to a world coping with the binary effects of invasion and the current reality of new colonialisms. I see how Native women are hurting so badly, tired of the same old things that keep them oppressed. When I take time to grieve our missing and murdered Sisters I just cry and cry and sing out these sad songs. Given everything that happened in my family, I say *wela'lin* to *Kisulk* that my own sisters and cousins found sanctuary. I also see how Native men are numb, unable to publicly express their feelings about what is going on and afraid of the consequence when they do, suffering in silence. Their hurts are so big. I see that men would like to be able to express their love for each other, showing their sensitivity, without others calling into question their sexualities or genders, nor relying on homo/transphobia to deflect their uncomfortability. When I want to be close to another man, it isn't because we are "gay", it is because we see in each other something beautiful, fresh and, at the same time, old. Sometimes this is sexual; other times it is just warmth. These hurts and divisions are not the big picture but close observations of a person who is actively working to heal these wounds in our communities and I know there is much more to who we are. We are radiant, powerful beings who remember. We are tender hearts with fierce fists fighting back at how our lives have been controlled and manipulated by invasion. We are lovers who sway like sweetgrass in the wind and cleanse when lit with the fires of longing.

The conditions of my training as a Two-Spirit person are certainly different than they were four or seven generations ago, but the knowledge within me is the same and interpretation is partially of my own choice. I understand that my ancestors made the best decisions they could, given the circumstances of their lives. I have learned that our/my ancestors lived through horrendous violence. It isn't our fault.

My family thinks me "crazy" for asking questions about the gaps in our stories. What they don't realize is that effects of these omissions are still alive within me; I am nothing without this knowledge. These legacies of historical trauma, doled out by the invading system will not go unnoticed or untransformed in this body. I work them every day, finding ways to soothe the immense losses stuck in these bones. Forgiveness is still a ways off. Acceptance, however, is wrapped up in this medicine bundle of contradictions. I am learning to enjoy how I am free to move and breathe. My medicine is bound with this knowledge, being many things all at once, assisting me to grieve what I and we have lost in getting here, while we grow something new together. I am hopeful for this process of un-settling we have begun.

* * *

Louis Esme Cruz *(Mi'kmaq/Acadian + Irish) BFA, is currently living on Three Fires Territory as a free agent. He happily collaborates and supports the Native Youth Sexual Health Network, the Aboriginal Youth Harm Reduction Project at YouthCO AIDS Society and Redwire Native Youth Media Project. His writing will appear in the upcoming* Sovereign Erotics: A Collection of Two-Spirit Literatures.

Internal War, Woven Basket Shaking, A Purple and Green Line Moving in Opposite Directions, Crisp Early Morning

FOUR POEMS BY NIMIKII COUCHIE

My name is Nimikii Couchie. I am loon clan from Nipissing First Nation. I am 16 and attend Widdifield Secondary School. I recently started writing poetry. I've grown a love and passion for poetry. For as long as I can remember I've loved to write.

For me writing is a personal expression of who I am. I have studied singing, acting, and dancing in school and with my parents, who are both professional artists. More recently I've began studying writing with my grandmother Lee Maracle who is also a professional artist and an honorary doctorate.

Currently my focus is on dance and writing poetry. On occasion I play keyboard and violin. I would like to make violin and piano a higher priority.

My goals and dreams have always provided me with a positive outlook on my future. I have a strong, clear sense of where I am headed and never give up. I value trying your best at everything you strive to do, because I know that the little steps along the way make the big steps possible.

* * *

Internal War

Thoughts run through my head
jumping back and forth
back and forth.
I don't know where I stand.
Frustration. Frustration
Where am I going?
I let it out.
It's too much for me to hold.
Tension and discomfort
Relax, relax, dilute the feeling.
Stand inside your walls,
Find your ground.
Stand inside your walls of importance

Woven Basket Shaking

My lower body and mind is completely free.
My lower back and upper back sink into the floor.
The bottoms of my feet are exposed
I can feel the air in the room.
I get a shivering, shaking feeling in my right shoulder.
As I feel this sensation,
the image of the woven basket shaking emerges.
The items shake inside the basket;
Sliding and moving almost like they are trying to escape.
The basket wants to stop shaking,
so it can feel the release of tension

A Purple and Green Line Moving in Opposite Directions

My eye lids flutter.
I look at the clear orange background.
I take two soft inhalations and exhale
The orange background becomes still
Now I can see the two long lines of colour move
the top line is green
the bottom is purple
They move in opposite directions.
As I look at the lines of colour I hear a continuous high, pitch beep
sound
It reminds me of when the TV. Station shuts down
all you can see are lines of colour
all you can hear is a high pitched beep
It reminds me of the state of being completely free from life
free from thoughts.

Crisp Early Morning

From up above the crow throws his berries at me.
I lay down beneath the crow
trying to relax,
The bird continues to throw his berries at me,
i jolt, feeling startled,
I feel the cool breeze on the bottoms of my feet,
on the left side of my face I feel the chill wind
from beneath me I feel the cold fresh ground hold me up,
up above the crow continues to throw his berries,
twitching, but struggling to ignore him
the annoying sound gets more violent,
the bird looks angry,
he gets louder and louder and continues to repeat,
He will not stop till I show my anger,
He gets louder and louder and continues to repeat,
He will not stop till I show my discomfort,
He feeds off my anger,
but I will not engage

AQSAzine: Muslims Speaking for Ourselves

AQSAzine (est. 2007) is a Toronto-based grassroots art collective by and for young women and trans people who self-identify as Muslim. Our main project is the creation of annual 'zine of writing, art, activism entitled AQSAzine. This zine is a creative avenue for young Muslim women and trans people to express ourselves, share our experiences and connect with others.

Salam! AQSAzine (est. 2007) is a Toronto-based grassroots arts collective of young women and trans people who self-identify as Muslim. Our main project is the creation of an annual 'zine of our writing, art and activism, also entitled *AQSAzine*. The 'zine is a creative avenue for us to express ourselves, share experiences and connect with others. We strive to work from an explicit anti oppressive, pro-choice, queer positive & trans positive framework. www.aqsazine.com.

In Arabic, the word "AQSA" means "reaching out to the furthest possible point" and AQSAzine aims to motivate the utmost resistance to oppression in all its forms. Aqsa Parvez was a 16-year-old whose life was taken on December 10, 2007. Our work is to honour her and all Muslim women and trans people who experience and resist violence. Jerusalem's Masjid A-Aqsa in Palestine is also an inspiration to us because of its associations with Prophet Muhammad (SBUH)'s ascension (also known as the "night of Isra and Miraj"). We strive to work from an explicit anti-oppressive, pro-choice, queer positive & trans positive framework.

The AQSAzine collective is made up of individuals with extremely diverse relationships to Islam (which loosely means "submission to God"). We know that Muslims are not a static monolithic group, and recognize that Islam can and does exist in various forms in each of our lives. It can manifest itself in ways that are spiritual, political, cultural and/or familial. We're also aware that while some of us ungrudgingly call ourselves "Muslim", others are sometimes forced to wear this label. Our work is educational; it is an ongoing dialogue about the issues young Muslim women and trans people are facing. Rather than having our identity constantly defined by others, we offer a platform to engage with our issues and offer new perspectives that reflect the complexity of our identities. This creative forum is where we inspire each other to keep questioning and growing into ourselves.

We aim to highlight our own stories, triumphs, and tragedies — to stop explaining ourselves or rationalizing our existence but, rather, to congregate, share, and learn. Our intention is not to impose our beliefs on anyone else, but simply to share some of our stories — stories that are complex and not always heard.

We refuse under any circumstances to pigeonhole ourselves and believe that is the true nature of diversity. We speak for ourselves individually under the umbrella of the idea of "aqsa", pushing beyond limits to discover who we are. It's a journey, not a conclusion, and we all get a say in where we're going. Below are some examples of this. Read, enjoy and join us.

Peace, love and hugs,
AQSAzine Team

"...most gracious, most merciful"
By Azza Abbaro

Sudanese by passport and a citizen-of-the-world by choice, **Azza Abbaro** was born and raised in various parts of the Middle East. Succumbing to a lingering need for creative expression wherever she went, she moved to Canada in 2003 to pursue an Hon. BSc in Visual Studies from the University of Toronto. Azza's creative vision is to translate the work of individuals, organizations, and grassroots movements into the appropriate media to help to raise awareness, generate dialogue, and inspire positive action. She is the Co-Founder and Art Director for AQSAzine. Azza remains a nomad at heart and hopes to continue this work wherever in the world she goes.

Oysian, Chimurenga, puradchi.....

BY GOLSHAN ABDMOULAIE

I walked for miles to get here
I never thought I would live here
What is this place you have promised me?
What is this dream that doesn't acknowledge me?
Questions that arise
People lookin' mesmerized
Will someone please summarize?
"You can't bring them here"
"There is nothing you can do or say"
"They will be raped and scared'
"Please sir there has to be something I could do"
"Someone please help me... help them"
"You can't bring them here, there is nothing you can do or say"
So I say
Walked for miles to get here
I never thought I would live here
What is this place you have promised me?
What is this dream that doesn't acknowledge me?
Questions that arise
People lookin' mesmerized
Will someone please summarize?
This is too hard for me, can't you see
I live here in western "democracy"
And they live there in eastern "theocracy"
Faith mixed with confused ideologies,
Young women trapped in all the hypocrisy
When did we become the powerless ones??
When we are the powerful ones who held up kingdoms
And fought 2 for freedoms
"Osysian, Chimugrenga, puradchi"
WHEN DID WE BECOME THE POWERLESS ONES
Stop
Tip toe...gracefully, quietly, calmly, delicately
Stop
Speak no loud words, don't smoke that cigarette, cross your legs, and
wipe off your nails
Stop

Pull up your top, cover your ass and make sure you never sway your
hips
Stop
Acid in the face
Stop
Acid in the face
Stop
Now no one will ever want you
Stop
Now no one will ever marry you
Now you must carry you
So I say
I walked for miles to get here
I never thought I would live here
What is this place you have promised me?
What is this dream that doesn't acknowledge me?
Questions that arise
People lookin' mesmerized
Will someone please summarize?
Southern and Northern ties
Western and Eastern Lies
None of your dreams fit me
NONE OF YOUR DREAMS FIT ME!!!!!
So I march for my freedom singing...
"Osysian, Chimugrenga, puradchi"

* * *

Golshan Abdmoulaie *is an Iranian Canadian; she came to Canada
when she was seven. After graduating from York University she began
to work as a youth counselor with refugee and immigrant youth using
arts as a mean of engagement and empowerment. Poetry has always
been her method for self expression, healing and giving voice to
issues that are often silenced.*

A rant: Ya si sayed
BY GHADEER M.

Si sayed is a character created by Naguib Mahfouz (Egyptian writer and Nobel prize winner) to embody the characteristics of a traditional Egyptian man in the 70s. This figure for me reflects elements of patriarchy that I found to exist in various contexts and places, and in different male figures in my life. I wrote this rant in response to those figures but especially because I see patriarchy as the backbone for other systems of oppression such as racism, capitalism, and colonialism.

Ya si sayed,

Symbol of patriarchy, master of the home and state alike,
I've been holding a lot of anger for you recently, so let me take this opportunity to introduce myself:

I am woman, I am strong and I do what I want.

My mind is just as much mine as is my body
My heart is just as much mine as are my choices.
My life is just as much mine as yours is yours.

And simply because of that...we have a problem.

You treat women as if you own us. superior to us and inherently stronger. Convinced some that your control is out of devout, love, compassion, and faith. But what's honest about holding our bodies captive to your wills and desires? what's loving about the leash you've put on mothers, wives, sisters and daughters? Taking choices away from us, decisions that are rightfully ours.

For a long time I was confused about why there was different standards for women than for men. why sex for me is shameful and for you masculine. why you hold me accountable for families, children, your culture pride and honor. while you walk out dusting one shoulder at a time without once thinking about who's honor you've got tangled up in the empty spaces between your fingers. mine or yours? why your sick cravings are justified, satisfied, delivered while I cradle in pockets of self-hate, a footstool for your guilt and mine.

You want everything that is mine. defined love with parameters that wrap up around you, fragments of darkness you've housed me in. you think you have a right over the times when unconditional love was only a duty of mine; the times I didn't know where you end and I begin.

Fuck you. I'm angry now. you've claimed my individuality, will and independence. robbed me from education, sex and a job, from my right to make my own mistakes, follow my instincts and run with my heart.

So let me lay down a few ground rules...

First, my body is mine, I use it the way I want and I do whatever I want with it. When I stand tall it means I've come further than you – I've not only seen through your lies but I've also won your war.

Second...and this is very important so listen well, my sexuality is not yours to define, label, take away or express. It is not yours to say who I am sleeping with, when and how. Marriage or no marriage. Women or man and trans.

Finally, I have my own will. you've created gender, stereotypes of what a woman and what a man is. haven't you learned already that human expression does not lie on two ends of a spectrum? haven't you learned already that there is no spectrum, that nothing fits tightly into boxes, that your constructions have failed?

You imagine the world is at your feet and that you sit on some kind of ostentatious throne. Entitles to this fictitious place, you kick off your shoes, stretch your feet; belly dangling, hair growing out of your ears, and watch below at the monuments you are creating:

Systems constructing structures informing diligent minion minds hard at work. Governments designing a mode of behavior, systemizing forms and categories of discrimination, sorting through colours and sizes — purposefully exclusive — you ask us all to take our place in your kingdom.

High-rises will fall short of your sight when they crumble and fall. Just as we speak.
Because we speak, cracking open conspiracies of motivations hiding deep in places that you don't event seek.

Insecure about your power, hungry for more, you throw a fit, feet in the air and scream out loud hoping to drown out the voices of objections, questions and inquiries.

Listen to me — no longer will you allow yourself to tell me what to do. What to cover or not cover, what messages my body will carry for you.

Things are going to change around here.

And I know that you are afraid, and that your violence only fosters because of shame of your own mistakes.

But so you should be...
Trimble and quiver from the thought of your cold fate approaching you.
Then sit still and surrender as the chaos from soles rubbing on pavements and streets turn into rubble and settle lightly on the shoulders of your pride.

Alone and desolate...like all captured kings.
Dethroned, de-powered. Ropes cut through your throat.

You've lost.
Because I'm woman – and I do what I want.

* * *

Ghadeer M. *is a feminist Palestinian activist living in Toronto. She is passionate about poetry and spoken word and lives her life with the goal of ending the colonization of Palestine and liberating women.*

An Open Letter

Do we expect betrayal in each other's gaze, or recognition — *Audre Lorde*

* * *

Dear Sisters,

This is a call to action.

We are the outcast, the not-Muslim-enough non-hijab-wearing, short-haired, short-skirted, supposedly-sexually-active sister at the back of the mosque feeling the burning eyes on the back of our heads as we enter a room filled with our ummah. We are also the niqab-wearing, hijab-wearing, supposedly-oppressed/oppressive sister in your class ignored and pushed aside for not being seen as "feminist" enough.

What we are asking for is simple: RESPECT. That same respect we give to you. We stand up for your rights without hesitation because we believe that they are an extension of our rights. We support your right to exist and express yourself. Yet it seems as if it is an imposition — even offensive — that we ask you to hear and acknowledge our stories, our lived experiences.

Backbiting is an offense in Islam, yet it is daily employed by each of us to police, to persecute and punish one another for supposed transgressions. After the racism, xenophobia, sexism and other forms of oppression we receive daily, the last thing we need is to worry about community members hating on us. The only judge is Allah, after all.

We see you when we speak out at events and instead of hearing our words you are giving our clothing the once-over. Your false judgments of us close your ears to what we have to say or, worse, twist our words and confessions to use as ammunition against us. We know when we are shunned at community events, told that we are unmarriageable, that it might very well have to do with what others, namely you, have said. It is a strain for us to have to edit ourselves in your presence so we can be included and accepted in spaces that are supposed to be our own.

We hear you when you snicker in the back of class when we are presenting, calling us non-Muslims because of our social locations. This tension that we feel when we enter a room filled with our Muslim sisters hurts and weighs heavy on our backs. Should we not be helping one another build and grow?

We feel your racism when you put us down because we are from nations that are not yours. Our beloved communities should be places of refuge not ones in which we have to shield ourselves from discrimination.

Being Muslim is about unity, hope and light. We are not asking you to extend yourself to some impossible task, we are asking you to meet us half way and from there we can work together. Our common enemy is ignorance, injustice and oppression, it is not one another. Let's stop judging, assuming and hating on each other. We hope it doesn't take further attacks on our Muslim communities for you to support us but we will take you any way you come. When violence happens to one of you, be it systemic or community based, we will be there. We hope the same can be said of you.

Peace,
Your Sister

* * *

The "Introduction" and "Dear Sisters" were written by AQSAzine Collective, which strives to work from an explicit anti oppressive, pro-choice, queer positive & trans positive framework. www.aqsazine.com.

SHABIKI CRANE

Pride From Behind

We've had a tumultuous relationship; my backside and me. Whenever I think we've reached an agreement I realize that we really haven't at all. Growing up we endured malicious school yard taunts, dreaded shopping trips, envy, unwanted touching and attention by men and women alike.

I happened to have inherited my ample behind from my ancestors from West Africa. Some call it a blessing, while others would say it was definitely a curse. Depending on the day, I could agree with either sentiment. Nonetheless we have endured it all together; my backside and me. I thought that feminism would save me from all this. Save me from years of growing up in an environment where sexuality and shame were considered pretty much the same thing. Looks like it didn't.

As a teenager my view of feminism was optimistic and idealistic. It was celebrating "equal pay, for equal work," burning bras, and protesting. It was supposed to unite all women for the same cause. Us against them, because as women we were taught that we are all subjected to the same inequality. So of course we could all fight the same battle, right? However, I quickly learned that certain "battles" could only be fought by me alone.

In high school I was summoned to the guidance office by the

77

counsellor regarding my pants. As most students who attended my uniform-wearing Catholic school, we all made our feeble attempts to assert our individuality through renouncing the proper uniform while substituting some of our own personality. I, like many girls I knew, chose to wear tight-fitting grey pants as opposed to the ugly, baggy, and shapeless pants from the uniform store. I remember checking myself numerous times in the mirror; I looked good! Unfortunately, it was not a mutual opinion. The guidance counsellor coyly explained to me that I shouldn't wear tight pants because "people would think badly of me". He even went as far as to say that Asian and white girls could get away with it because of their shapes, but on me it only looked vulgar. I felt vulgar.

Black women are often considered to be "sexually deviant" or beings lacking respect for themselves. After all we have all seen those "disgusting rap videos" apparently while only a few people have viewed any 80's rock videos where blonde women can be seen crawling on cars, swinging around poles, or scampering around in those "skimpy" outfits. It often seemed as if only certain people had the right and privilege to use their sexuality in a manner that was perceived as "light-hearted" and fun, which was a power that was beyond the reach of the black rappers and the females who exist in their music videos. These women are often condemned or pitied for having so little "decency" by society. Yet, those who are repulsed were rarely willing to champion everyday beauty in black women. This incident (with my guidance counsellor) only reinforced my own feelings of guilt and shame, believing that if I received any unwanted attention it was due to assumptions out of my own control.

I took one women's studies class in my first year university, and found that I couldn't really relate with much of the material. It was from such a white middle class perspective. Women from other cultures were always presented as victims as in, "Poor, poor Muslim women who cover their heads — we are so lucky that we live where we live and believe what we believe."

Colonialism was rarely mentioned, and when it was most of my white classmates complained of reverse-racism, expecting me to "back them up." When I didn't one girl asked me, "Why can't you just accept that they won and stop using it as an excuse for everything; frequent pregnancies and poor education, etc."

Leading me to wonder: was I? Was I conquered? When I wore "sensible, modest clothing" was I conquered because I had bought into the myth of what a decent black woman looked like? Or, was I conquered if I dressed "scandalously." Perhaps I was simply conquered because I cared about how I would be perceived?

Either way, I was truly "done" with women's studies after my professor announced to the class that when white women like Britney Spears presented themselves in a sexual manner it was because they were asserting their sexuality; however, when black women, like Beyonce did, they were simply being puppets and degrading themselves. I couldn't understand the way that both images wouldn't invoke the same reaction regardless of whether it was seen as empowerment or degradation, but why not the same? I saw two women singing, shaking, shimmying and to my horror, recognized that it would never be the same. It just reiterated the feelings of dis-empowerment I had harboured throughout the years of my life.

Feminism dictates that women deserve to be equal to men, but the truth is it's telling us that some women are more deserving than others. Like at my dance recital fitting when I was five, I was given a dress with "flesh colour" material around the neck. It was beige, I am dark brown; I noticed. For me, feminism (in academia) just seems like another place where there is no room for me. So now I continue to rediscover that it's about finding my own place to take, and refusing to be placed.

* * *

Shabiki Crane *is a writer of children's content. She is an avid traveller, a wandering theorist, and a defeatist humanist. She finds the restrictions of society alarming, but is willing to find her own way around them.*

Male Feminist and Invisible Activists

TWO POEMS BY
ROBERT ANIMIKII HORTON

Male Feminist

As an Indigenous, First Nation, male activist, I am often asked what does being a "male feminist" mean to me?

It means equality rather than superiority by either side, in every context, and living the value of respect infused with that precious equality.

To me, it means being willing to open one's eyes and heart to the fact that, in our age of purported civic integrity and opportunity, massive inequality exists between men and women, and that much work must be done so our collective walk matches our collective talk.

To me, it means we all have a place in the sacred circle; men and women. Young and old.

To me, it means understanding that our personal, intellectual, emotional, and spiritual selves are both masculine and feminine, both leaders and nurturers, each rooted and grown skyward with strength and resiliency, not accepting sharpened extremes, but rather a million shades of grey in between.

To me, it means holding the utmost respect towards Two-Spirited persons who stand strong among those million degrees of distinction.

To me, it means understanding that because respect that is endemic to our Indigenous culture, abuse and superiority over women is incompatible with claims of "Native Pride."

To me, it means acknowledging the history in which patriarchy and deplorably-imposed institutional religion have affected respect, balance, and conduct towards women.

To me, it means not only holding this awareness within, but spreading awareness and working to deconstruct and dismantle inequality in the short time we are given in our lives.

To me, it means understanding that, traditionally, if women were acknowledged as the center of our families and as our life-givers, and if our Nations still stand, then women are the center of our Nations and the future of the same.

To me, it means understanding before we can take to the streets as activists, step to the podium as orators, imagine that we are progressives or agents of change, or challenge the power structures of inequality in our society, we must examine if our own conduct, ideologies, and actions truly stand for that same equality in our own households, in our communities, and in our workplaces with our sisters, mothers, daughters, partners, elders, and life givers (from any place, background, or heritage) in our own lives.

To our leaders: to our Brothers AND Sisters: May we "Walk Our Talk" on every level — from our homes to our cause.

So, as an Indigenous, First Nation, male activist, what does being a male feminist mean to me?

This means, in a word, pure and simple: Integrity.

Invisible Activists

This is a statement to honour and express gratitude to the single mothers of our world who make it a point to serve as both mothers and fathers to their children; who selflessly put in long hours on little sleep so their children will see brighter days and more opportunities. For many years, I was raised by my Mother, Shirley Ann Horton-Kampa (Niyoobinesik). This work was birthed of such gratitude and served as a means for me to say "Miigwech", but its genesis is equally in honoring those who follow similar footsteps; yesterday, today, and tomorrow.

With the words and faces of King and Goldman still stirring in
the air
Have we forgotten our nearest voices in the struggle that too
many share?
As the voices of Guevara, Malcolm, Parks, and Davis echo to our
day
Do we strain our eyes to see the invisible activists who follow in
their wake?
With the reminisce of Trudell, Steinem, Bellecourt, and Teters
lighting serrated roads
Where are the vigils for those, standing strong, in the path of
struggles bestowed?

Beside the legacies of Newton, Anna Mae, Seale, and Peltier,
Of Chavez, Marcos, and Banks
There are voices in our day, so silenced
And so overdue of honor, praise and thanks.

Our single mothers, radical subversives to the uphill climb
Arthritic, hardworking hands embrace seven cents instead of a
brother's wage-given dime
Higher learning, fatigued and yearning through the eighty hour
week
Boycotting paths of least resistance and the silent household
mystique
Speaking the words to build up her children to question the
common road
Civil disobedience to a virile social code

A podium of irony between awaiting ears at night-time stories,
But hushed to the core at workplace noontime theme
Pressing time and breath fogging the glass ceiling above
But cleaning it away for her children to look up and dream

Have we forgotten the activists who truly make the time?
That struggle uphill and who keep the hope sublime?
Have we forgotten the leaders that lead us through and guide
With one set of footsteps, not two, which walk along our side?
Do we remember the reformer, the advocate, the militant, and
her dream?
The revolutionary, the radical, the outspoken and her regime?
Do we remember all of these, all existent in her gaze
Before the everyday strikes and protests so we may see better
days?

Through a single mother's eyes — our dreams; our lives may
become.
Through an invisible activist's reach — we have overcome.

* * *

Robert Animikii Horton (Bebaamweyaazh) *is a Anishinaabe and Suomea member of Rainy River First Nations from the Anishinaabe Marten Clan. He is a sociologist, dedicated writer, social analyst, international orator, social/political activist, and spoken-word poet. Horton was raised in Minnesota and calls International Falls, MN home.*

MEGAN LEE

"Maybe I'm not Class-Mobile; Maybe I'm Class-Queer"
Poor kids in college, and survival under hierarchy

As a kid from a lower-class home who was privileged enough to attend university, I spent two years in women's studies classrooms watching the same token superficial analyses of racism and classism get regurgitated over and over again. Few academics that I encountered were comfortable or even conscious enough to deal with the ways that university works as a mechanism to perpetuate class hierarchy. I was not an ideal candidate to broach the subject either — as a poor kid, I was in that classroom precisely to get myself out of the lower-class social group that I had been a part of my whole life. If I spoke up against the classist aspects of the academic industry and the values that permeate it, I knew that I would be attacking everyone in the classroom, including myself. I didn't know if my thoughts were rational or if they were simply the product of misplaced resentment, and I didn't know if I could even speak for a group that I was in the process of trying to escape. I lay low for a long time.

Getting educated didn't just entail a change in my C.V. and prospective earnings; the institution and the student body were permeated by a value-set and worldview that pressured me to alter my language, my appearance, the elements of my personal background that I learned to conceal, the values that I was expected to hold, my relationships, my alliances, my family ties, and my identity as a person. My women's studies classes were supposed to be a respite and a support, a place where I could voice my uneasiness with the institution and where I could sort out these conflicted ideas. Instead, I was met with slight-of-hand, apologist pandering, and dismissal. Wherever I tried to raise the issue, it was acknowledged briefly but the discussion quickly shifted before anything meaningful was said. Academic institutions reinforced class privilege, but academic feminism, for all its espoused anti-oppressive commitments, did not want to get into the details.

For a while, I kept my personal life a complete secret. The fact that my immediate family was on social assistance was something that was not to be talked about if I was to accomplish the transformation from poor to not-poor. To mark myself as different was to raise the issue that class privilege is not merely a social starting-point established at birth, but perpetuated and reconstructed at every moment of our lives. Being in university made us complicit in the reconstruction and perpetuation of class hierarchy. The issue was not one of blame — who could blame someone for not wanting to live in poverty? But it still tasted bitter. Nobody wanted to talk about it.

At home, though, it was impossible to ignore the fact that I was going to school while my family members were on social assistance or working low-paying manual labour jobs — my education tested and transformed my relationships with my family. We talked often about what it meant for me to "move up" in terms of class, to "leave this life behind." My mother had always pushed me to achieve as much as I could, so that I would not have to suffer the degradations that she had, living in poverty; however, as I began to put down roots in the middle-class professional world, it became clear that there was a lot of unresolved, even unacknowledged tension and anger with regard to those with class privilege. We had not constructed this "us and them" world, but we had lived in it all of our lives, and suddenly, I was becoming a "them."

My mother is sometimes afraid that I will become privileged and that I will internalize the classist values that paint her as a failure, a loser, a welfare bum, and a "bad mother." She sometimes feels pain and jealousy because I have so many opportunities that she never had. She sometimes feels abandonment, because I am inhabiting realms of experience that she has always been situated on the outside of. She used to go through cycles of resentment because she feared that I would become like the many privileged young professionals in public interest fields who claim to understand the experience of being oppressed by virtue of their education and rely on the authority of their education to silence and ignore the actual experiences of oppressed people. In contrast, there were times when she wanted to cut off all contact with me because she was afraid that my ties to my family would "drag me down" and prevent me from living an easier life. Every fierce, complex, and conflicted emotion that she has felt towards me, I have also felt towards myself. We are still in the process of sorting it all out.

The personal/political exercise of self-examination and communication that my family and I are engaged in is the main site on which my feminism is practiced. I re-read Andrea Smith's piece on white supremacy, which (among other things) talks about rethinking the concept of family as something that unites diverse members with complicated relationships to one another. This idea resonated with me at a profound level, since my relationship with my family has been the main force guiding my feminism. Growing up, my single mom struggled to keep my brother and me fed, clothed, and safe from an abusive father, and to give us the kind of foothold in the world that she herself had never had. She fought her whole life to survive, and that spirit of tooth-and-nail survivalism permeated my childhood and is the bedrock of my feminist convictions. I was raised with the understanding that in this upward battle, it is not only our bodies but our minds and identities that must endure and remain whole.

In my family, we are diverse individuals who occupy distinct social locations, but we are deeply invested in the survival of the whole. We are a family of hapas; our roots are Chinese, Black, Western-European and Native. I have always been able to pass as white, and my white privilege has significantly affected the academic, social and professional circles that I have been a part of. Unlike the rest of my family, I have the safety and luxury of being racially invisible when I choose to be. I am privileged by the same racist systems that oppress my mother and my brother; at the same time, my brother is privileged by heteronormative patriarchal systems that subordinate me as a lesbian. Ignoring these dangerous dynamics is not an option — not for my family, and not for any human being who wishes to participate in the creation of an anti-oppressive movement. We need to understand these mechanisms of oppression in order to understand and love one another.

My family has been engaged in a loving, open dialogue about difference for years, and at this moment, we have never been stronger — as individuals or as a unit. But it took a lot of work and energy on all sides to keep this dialogue going and to keep our family strong. It took a lot of openness that was, more often than not, painful for everyone involved. We were lucky that our relationship was strong enough at the outset, that our ties to one another were able to survive the crush of poverty, sexual abuse, assault, drugs, mental illness, and repeated brutalizing hospitalization. We were lucky that our efforts to listen and self-examine were able to produce such positive growth. There were many, many times when I thought that our family would not survive, when I was forced to leave my home because of conflict, when I wanted to drop out of school completely, and when I felt like my identity and what I thought was my family and my home had been shattered into a million irreparable pieces.

From talking to the few-and-far-between university students from poor backgrounds that I've encountered, don't think that my experience is idiosyncratic. Poverty is not simply having no money — it is isolation, vulnerability, humiliation and mistrust. It is not being able to differentiate between employers and exploiters and abusers. It is contempt for the simplistic illusion of meritocracy — the idea that what we get is what we work for. It is knowing that your mother, with her arthritic joints and her maddening insomnia and her post-traumatic stress disordered heart, goes to work until two in the morning waiting tables for less than minimum wage, or pushes a janitor's cart and cleans the shit-filled toilets of polished professionals. It is entering a room full of people and seeing not only individual people, but violent systems and stark divisions. It is the violence of untreated mental illness exacerbated by the fact that reality, from some vantage points, really does resemble a psychotic nightmare. It is the violence of abuse and assault which is ignored or minimized by police officers, social services, and courts of law. Poverty is conflict. And for poor kids lucky enough to have the chance to "move up," it is the conflict between remaining oppressed or collaborating with the oppressor.

I live in a province where university tuition is extremely subsidized (I pay about $3,000 a year for my law degree) and where need-based financial aid is mostly available. Yet I can count on one hand the number of poor kids that I have met in university. Financial barriers to education are a serious issue, and I do not wish to minimize the importance of fighting for accessible education — however, it is not enough on its own. The fight for accessible education has to be a panoramic fight against poverty — against dehumanization, ghettos, exploitation, and fear. It needs to be the fight for anti-racist collectives and radical immigration reform, and it needs to be the fight against the non-profit industrial complex wherein some organizations, under the guise of anti-oppressive activism, re-enforce the status of the privileged (for they are the educated professionals) and remain invested in the oppression of the poor and racialized (for they are the "clients" who legitimize the non-profit organization.) The fight for accessible education has to seek to change universities from institutions that reinforce oppressive hierarchies to institutions that break oppressive hierarchies down.

From my own experience, I feel that separatism in a world of oppression is not sufficient to create justice — at least, with regards to class-oppression. In fact, systems of privilege benefit from separatism because they allow the privileged to persist in their justificatory narrative without being troubled by the rage of those whose backs their privilege is built upon. The current model of "class-mobility" reinforces separatism and class-hierarchy because it posits that in order to escape oppression, one must become an oppressor — and universities do not merely mediate the boundary between professional and labourer, they teach the body of knowledge, the worldview, the values that mark a person as professional, as "belonging" to the middle- or upper-class.

Universities teach us to renounce our sense of identification with the poor; they teach this by mainly ignoring the existence of poor people, and by treating us as "other" when we do become the subject of discussion. Universities teach us not to care too much, because it will undermine our professional role. Universities teach us that we are separate from where we came from, that we are "qualified" (which suggests that our families and peers are not), that we are justified in having power over people, in speaking for the subjects of our study. Universities teach us that we are "too good" to wait tables and clean houses, with the implication that those who do those jobs are "not good enough" to deserve better.

Poor people tend to see university as a way out for their kids, but university is also a way in to the class of people whose success is premised on the oppression of the poor. In the course of my upbringing, I was exposed to a lot of conflicted ideas surrounding university and class mobility. "Moving up" was seen as both highly desirable and worthy of derision and scorn. It was the subject of envy, resentment and outright hatred. Some of the black kids on my block got called "white" for reading books; it made sense, since the educated professionals whose houses were cleaned and whose children were reared by lower-class people of colour were mostly white. Education had a strong class and race connotation to it, and contrary to what most privileged people tend to think, going to college was not something that evoked uncomplicated positive feelings in most of the poor people I knew, myself included. For a kid to become educated meant that he or she would live an easier life that was premised on the oppression and invisibility of the very communities s/he came from. This left a foul taste in many mouths.

I have had that foul taste in my mouth for years, and I have come to the provisional conclusion that it is the taste of injustice — of being forced to choose between the indignity of remaining poor and the ethically repellant strategy of privilege-seeking. To a poor kid who has the chance to go to college or university, participating in an institution that she identifies as oppressive (either before attending or in the course of her education) might seem like the best choice with regards to her survival, but it is a conflicted survival.

University is a classist institution — not only in the sense that financial barriers render it inaccessible to most poor people but in the sense that the culture of university imposes a homogeneous set of classist values, including dangerous delusions of meritocracy. My experience of women's studies in particular has been deeply alienating since the program claims "fighting oppression" as one of its objectives. Ideas about justice and empowerment that had been my tools of survival were present in our course materials, but they were rendered so abstract, and they were so dissociated from their real-world application that they were barely recognizable. Issues of racism and classism were identified as "problematic" and left at that. I found myself in a classroom sitting next to a blonde girl who raised her hand to complain that she didn't know how to talk to black people because she was uncomfortable with the idea that "they" might be hostile towards her. There were a couple of black women in the room, and I wish to god that I could transcribe their facial expressions because their faces said it all. Even when the oppressed person is sitting right there, the university setting permits everyone to talk about us in the third person.

Sometime during my fourth semester, I started ranting in seminars, arguing with professors after-hours, and disclosing my background to my peers. A few responded with respect and interest, but most responded with discomfort, disinterest, defensiveness, and anger. Of the former, most came from similar class backgrounds or had similar feelings of ambivalence and alienation within the university setting due to their race or cultural roots.

To talk with other people who are engaged in the same difficult task of working out the conflicts in their own narrative, I have started to imagine a new kind of interstitial identity: citizenship within no man's land. When we work together, we can go beyond the question of what university is doing to us, and we can start thinking about what we can do to the university. Academic institutions have the power to construct one group of people as "professional" or "qualified" and thus relegate everyone else to the status of "unqualified" — moreover, they are not about to lose this power anytime soon. But we can get a hold of some of that power, and we can control how it is used. We can change the internal composition of the institution by staying in school and getting more of our own people in. We can participate in the institution on our own terms rather than on theirs, and we can redefine what an educated professional looks and sounds like.

We can challenge what knowledge is seen as legitimate and what is seen as illegitimate. And most of all, we can identify the role of the university itself, and the way that it sustains class divisions, the way that it functionally excludes people based on their economic status, and the way that it alienates the few who make it through the cracks. Academic feminism belongs too much to the oppressive white educated-class culture that infuses academia as a whole, but it is the most logical place to begin asserting our presence. We need to speak up in order to make room — psychologically and intellectually — for the ones who come after us. We need to carry our roots with us, and not forget or whitewash where we come from.

Note

I've spent four years in university — first women's studies, now law school. There are still a good number of mornings that I wake up feeling like a *compradora* and I hate myself inside and out. (Because I am seen as a valuable enough prospect, my university and government collaborate to give me free psychiatric counseling, which helps — although I'd feel better if my family also had access to comparable care. But I digress.) I know that I am where I am largely due to my privilege. I did grow up far below the poverty line, I am a lesbian and a survivor of sexual abuse, and I suffer from mental illness. But I am also a Canadian citizen and a Quebec resident, meaning that I can access extremely cheap post-secondary education and extremely cheap health care, among other things. I look more-or-less white and I am cisgendered. I am highly privileged. While I believe I'm in a decent position from which to examine the relationship between class and education, I know that my ideas and my efforts to understand the systems we live are greatly enriched by other perspectives, and I invite dialogue.

* * *

Megan Lee is a writer and musician who is studying at the McGill Faculty of Law. Her interests include promoting access to justice and transforming academic space. She currently works with the McGill Legal Information Clinic, the McGill Law High School Outreach Program, and McGill's Community Law Group.

ANNA SAINI

Sex Work and Feminism
An interview with anna Saini
by Jessica Yee

anna Saini has lived many lives as a political scientist, radical activist and multi-media artist. She is based part-time in Detroit, Michigan. Her writing appears in Bitch Magazine, Diverse Voices Quarterly, Two-Bit Magazine, VOCES *and in the anthology* Colored Girls. *For more information and updates visit http://www.annasaini.com.*

Jessica Yee: First off I gotta ask you this: the title of this book, what comes to mind for you? What's this really about?

anna Saini: i think academia is an environment where "isms" like feminism are unchecked by real experiences. For instance, in graduate school we discussed ad nauseum the idea of "overlapping oppression" while we ignored the dynamics of sexism, racism, classism, ableism and other layers that shaped our experiences in the institution itself. As a result of these unchecked power dynamics between students, researchers, teachers and administrators — the power structure that is a determining factor in academia — much of what comes out of there is so biased and out of touch it lacks real world relevance.

i think this book is a part of a diverse movement of *real* people, people who survive the overlapping oppressions that "Feminism" attempts to address, taking action to reclaim and revive what feminism is really about. We are doing this by rejecting our roles as objects of study that are ascribed to us by the white capitalist academic complex, and placing ourselves and our lives at the center of research and theory.

This is the only way that feminism will regain relevance: by connecting theory to practice to action in the lives of regular people.

JY: Let's start talking about sex work and feminism. But first since we are indeed "deconstructing the academic industrial complex" here, what does the word "sex work" mean in your opinion?

aS: Sex work is work where a person gets paid for a sex act. This is actually much more broad then it sounds when you remember that "sex act" is not synonymous with "intercourse" nor does it imply that there is necessarily orgasm or even nudity involved. A sex act is defined more by context than anything else. For instance, having a man wash your dishes is not conventionally considered a sex act but is when it a pro domme is having their submissive do chores as part of their session. In contrast, just because someone orgasms doesn't make it a "sex act" per se, like if i jack-off on the phone with a customer service agent it doesn't make him a sex worker. Escorts are perhaps the best known sex worker but they represent just one small piece of the work that composes the sex industry, including strippers, porn starts, dommes, phone sex workers and a host of others. The pivotal part of the definition is in the economic exchange amongst consenting adults. Without mutual consent, we're talking about sexual assault; without economic exchange, we're talking about sexual relations. The intersection of the two is the realm of sex work.

JY: Tell us a little bit about yourself — what do people need to know about you when it comes to talking about feminism as a sex worker?

aS: i am a strong believer in the "nothing about us, without us" philosophy, meaning that i consider myself an expert on my own experience and seek to prioritize the voices of people who are likewise gaining meaning from expressing and acting on their own experiences. i co-produce a radio show called Frequency Feminisms — Womyn Powered

Radio (FF-WPR) on CKLN 88.1FM in Toronto where we bring real feminism, the issues that affect women in our communities, to the airwaves every week. i've worked as a community organizer on issues of labour rights, equality in higher education, drug policy reform, women's abuse and prison abolition and I completed a graduate degree from Canada's "ivy league" but ultimately i am disillusioned with unsustainable activism, non-profit, academic and radical work structured in a way that prevents those who experience oppression to take leadership in creating change. Although i have agency in deciding to pursue sex-work, i wouldn't say that sex-work is a free choice for me. It is one of very few viable options to support my lifestyle as a poor, dis/abled women of colour media-maker who is vocal on issues of racism, sexism and classism. Since taking on sex-work as a career i've self-published an anthology of poetry called *Colored Girls* featuring work by myself and nine other women of colour media-makers from Los Angeles to Cairo, i've attended the *Speak-Up Media Training* in New York City and the *Desiree Alliance Conference*, a national sex work conference in Las Vegas as a presenter on surviving and transgressing violence, where i was fated to meet you, Jessica. i also attended the *Voices of Our Nation* writing workshop sponsored by the University of San Francisco for emerging writers of colour and started work on a memoir. Amongst all of this i am writing, gaining publishing credits and healing my post-traumatic stress disorder (PTSD). i look forward to the day when money is not the primary determining factor in the trajectory of my life. Sex work makes this a possibility for me.

JY: Now I've had it to here with what I see as the "policing" or "gatekeeping" of feminism. As in, you can't be a "real" feminist if you x, y, z and I witness this so much when it comes to sex work and feminism — like when these so-called "women's organizations" make generalizations on behalf of all feminists (as if they even have permission to do so!) by saying things like "All feminists think sex work is wrong". Um, hello, sex workers ARE feminists and who gives who the right to decide what is or isn't the "right" feminism?! What do you think about this?

aS: i think the feminists who actually come out and say these things are making explicit the classism and racism that usually goes unsaid throughout the movement. It's obvious that mainstream feminism cannot address the realities of sex workers because 2nd wave, white, middle-class feminists are so out of touch with the issues of race and poverty that underscore our experiences. What they cannot understand, they discount, instead of ceding their control and leadership of the movement to play a supporting role empowering us to fight for our own self-determination.

JY: I guess what it comes down to it what we are witnessing is this "saving" versus "supporting" complex that some people seem to have – especially when it comes to sex work. As in, people wanting to "save" sex workers from something instead of actually supporting sex workers to do what they need to do for themselves — and often times using the cloak of their version of "feminism" to mask what their true intentions are to "save" people. I'd call that neo-colonialism actually. Thoughts?

aS: Appropriation runs so deep and is so problematic in feminist organizations that attempt to control our bodies, our economic survival and our sex lives by stigmatizing sex work. i agree that the missionary slant that feminist "saviors" of sex workers adopt is a modern form of colonialism. Sex workers are the contemporary Venus Hottentot for all the fascination that white feminists have with fetishizing our work. It's so difficult to make clear that in a big way sex work is not about sex at all, it's about money, it's about making it by financially when other options have run out or were inaccessible to begin with. If they really wanted to help, they would work to correct the racist, capitalist, ableist and patriarchal power structures that force too many women into sex work, but because they have stake in these structures they are willfully ignorant to this perspective.

JY: Anything else you would like to share with us?

aS: i don't think anyone is defined by what work they do for pay. In an ideal world "job" is synonymous with "passion". i can envision this world in my art and the work of those in my communities, but in the mean time we need to respect the rights of people to identify with what they love rather than how they survive financially. We need to see beyond the confines that white, capitalist, patriarchy place on our humanity. Deconstructing the academic industrial complex of feminism means that we revere the dignity of all people, not as sex workers or academics, but as a community members, artists, revolutionaries and survivors.

ANDREA PLAID

"No, I Would Follow the Porn Star's Advice"
A case study in educational privilege and kyriarchy*

***Kyriarchy:** a coined word by feminist theologian Elisabeth Schussler Fiorenza as a modification of the term patriarchy which elaborates intersecting structures of domination. The word is derived from the Greek words for "lord" or "master" (kyrios) and "to rule or dominate" (archein), and defines a system of "ruling and oppression" in which many people may interact and act as oppressor and oppressed. (borrowed from Wikipedia)*

From a thread on filmmaker Aishah Shahidah Simmons's Facebook page on The Academy not producing leaders but producing professors:

> I do feel that far too many feminists who've been through the bachelor's-and-beyond degrees tend to be the ones who get — or feel entitled to — the mic based on that, including in sex-positive feminism. I've seen the shade thrown at those without master's degrees in women's studies/queer theory/sexology get thrown some serious shade by those who have the degree(s) or, more insidiously, those degrees don't come from Ivy-League or otherwise first-tier U.S. colleges and universities. Add to this the whole race/gender/ability thing, and it's a mess.

My response:

Hmmm...I'm struggling with this very problem in a piece for an anthology I'm working on about the feminism-academic complex. What I've found quite often is, from adjunct to tenured professors, that quite a few believe that not only they are inherently radical because they're professors (something about how radical "cultivating the next generation of minds" is) but their reading and researching loads makes them infallibly radical because they "know so much" about the topic they're being radical about. Then, to add to this, I've seen quite a few act as if, because they're degreed in one topic they're infallibly knowledgeable about a lot of topics. I've sat some academics down because they failed to simply read what I wrote.

But the thing is — and what rubs these academics the wrong way — is one doesn't need a degree to have a nuanced understanding or stance on a political or social issue or any intersection of those. (Latoya Peterson, owner/publisher of the race-and-pop-culture blog Racialicious instantly comes to my mind. She'll tell you that she's a college drop-out. Quite a few other publications for whom she's written will tell you she's a hellified in-demand writer. And, in full disclosure, she mentors my master's degree-having self. And no, she's not an exception to the rule.) And being degreed doesn't instantly guarantee a progressive mind — Charles Murray and his book, *The Bell Curve*, is one notorious example of that.

Here's how I see The Complex working, using myself as an example: I could have easily benefitted from the feminist-academic complex. I concentrated on women's studies as part of my liberal-arts degree and my Independent Study project when I was getting my master's degree in library science — since writing a master's thesis was not an option at the time — was on founding and operating a sex-positive library, though I did not specifically study sex as an undergrad or a graduate student. The fact that I have a bachelor's and master's degree allows me to be taken slightly more seriously because they signal that I know certain "privilege codes and signals" gotten from about seven years of beyond-high-school education, like knowing about or having the "right" books on my bookshelf or in my e-reader (Paulo Friere's *Pedagogy of the Oppressed*, Audre Lorde's *Sister*

Outsider, anything and just about everything by bell hooks, some Barbara Ehrenreich and Naomi Klein, etc.), having seen or heard about the right movies (anything Pedro Almodovar and Mira Nair, *Outfoxed*, *Matrix*, etc.) and the right music (usually some form of "alternative" hip-hop, rock, and country). It also means I know the "right" places to meet other like-minded educated people offline (coffee shops, poetry readings, film screenings, panel discussions, galleries and museums, and so on). In other words, my stating that I'm degreed lets others know that I'm the kind of "culturedness" that only a bachelor's and master's degree "can give" (translation: "can pay for" — which, really, is what educational privilege is welded with and signals)…and if I wasn't exposed to those things, I can damn sure learn it quickly because I know the "right" places to go to find such things, including the "right" Internet sources and from those adjunct and tenured types.

The linchpin in all of this and what I'm signalling to others by my degrees is that I'm capable of talking about complex ideas and issues, like the various schools of feminism, because I'm trained to do it based on the "virtue" of the "right" general knowledge and, furthermore, can take my complex notions to the "masses" who need to hear it and embrace it as part of their lives. (This notion is one of the rawest forms of educational privilege.) Because that, from what we're told in these social-class incubators called four-year colleges and advanced degrees, is the great responsibility that comes from the great advantage — and promise — of being an "educated person." The more subtle lesson passed to us in college is The Degreed are the only ones worth listening to — the more degreed, the more you're worth listening to because you're an "expert" due to all those years of studying. When feminists took the fight to make women's lives worth studying and analyzing to and within The Academy, that was one of the tenets that became absorbed and subsequently perpetuated, more often in various micro-aggressive ways, like rattling off where one went to school and "was an activist" in conversations at women's studies conferences or at the other aforementioned places to meet like-minded people.

But a couple of ideas fly in the face of that lesson, partly brought forth by feminism, particularly by feminists of colour: 1) the idea that each person is an expert on her own life and the lessons borne out of it and can speak on that; and 2) that the Internet allows some people to talk about their life expertise. In other words, one doesn't need a degree to talk about life, such as about sex.

And the sex-positive movement is fascinating because of the tension between The Degreed and the Self-Taught...over a blurry line. Sex-positivity rewards "Experience", such as the sex blogger who writes about her time as a sex worker (stripper, porn maker/actor, etc.) or, at least, about her sexual experiences in an effort to liberate herself from society's idea(l)s about women and gender and, by extension, trying to free the reader's mind and body, too. At the same time, some of the bigger "names" in sex-positivity, such as Carol Queen, Annie Sprinkle, and Audacia Ray, either have master's degrees or PhDs behind their names and/or come from credentialed sex institutes or from first-tier colleges and universities along with their experiences as sex workers and, by extension, are called on to expound on, say, the latest sex scandal. Even though quite a few "sexperts" are self-taught from learning what they know from non-college reading, having done sex work, and/or having done some sort of activism, a reality is that there are quite a few who do come from university-privileged backgrounds — and with university-privileged entitlement.

> **The sex-positive movement is fascinating because of the tension between The Degreed and the Self-Taught...over a blurry line.**

That's why, as much as I was shocked to see it go down, as much as I wanted to be supportive — in full disclosure, supportive of my friend — I simply wasn't. An example of what I mean...

Latina, the pop-culture and lifestyle magazine aimed at Latinas, announced in 2009 that porn star Ann Maria Rios would write a new sex-advice column called *Between the Sheets*.

I tweeted it as a news item...and a self-professed radical and Latina sexologist, Bianca Laureano, retweeted it with the rejoinder, "because there are no Latina sexologists." She just couldn't believe that the widely read publication just didn't find someone more qualified than Rios — like degreed, "professional" sexologists like, well, her.

That hiring Rios was more like stunt casting to get more eye-balls reading the publication than providing any sort of sorely needed sex advice for Latinas that a studied sexologist would be able to provide vis-à-vis obtaining a degree.

That *Latina* should have cast a wider net when they decided to create this position because, if they would've done so, they would have discovered many Latina sexologists willing to step in and write for them and not this...porn star. A couple of Laureano's friends recommended that she send her credentials to the publication.

Though Laureano wrote in a blog post that she "supports" Rios as a fellow sex professional and that perhaps *Latina* just may be setting her up for failure:

> I was/am hurt because I know that there are multiple ways to send messages. That *Latina Magazine* has power in our commu-nity with many of our members. How could they not find sexolo-gists in our community? Did they not find my website or the web-site of others in the field? I've shared that one of the things I long for is to be respected and acknowledged as the professional in the field that I am! It's been a struggle; seasoned sexologists have dis-missed me because of my age, ethnicity, or size (to name a few). To see Latina Magazine make a decision that ignored me, us, was the sting that led me to write this post.

> What message is *Latina Magazine* sending us when they hire a young Latina in the adult industry to lead a column on sex advice? What happens to the conversations about the sociological, psychological, anthropological, affects upon sexuality? What about when topics such as immigration, rape, incest, domestic vio-lence, abortion, miscarriage (and the D&C that may follow), build-ing relationships and having sex after such experiences come up?... Sexuality is far beyond the act of sex, or of exchanging bod-ily. The exchange of power, energy, consent, accountability, respon-sibility, and history is what sexuality also includes (again to name a few).

But from what I understand about the porn field, women do call the shots — have power, can give and refuse consent — as to which partners with whom they will have sex or, to use the lingo, "do a scene" and well as what sex acts they will do. Rios couldn't use that experience when giving answers about sexual consent and desire? And what she doesn't know about the anthropological/sociological/psychological couldn't Rios look it up online? She doesn't need an advanced degree to Google.

Furthermore, Laureano questions:

Is there an idea that AnnMarie is a safe choice because of her background and profession without regard for her sustainability in the field?

As a result, I think that AnnMarie will not find the support and respect she has earned and deserved as a successful Latina in the sexuality field, and I know all too well how this feels and would not wish this situation on anyone. My fear of this occurring to AnnMarie has already begun. Her expertise is being questioned (which I believe is appropriate to an extent), her character is being disrespected because she is a sex worker (which is juvenile), and people are already dismissing her (which cancels out *Latina Magazine*'s efforts right?).

I'd like to make this very clear: I'm on Ann Marie's side! I hope she gives *Latina Magazine* what they are looking for 100 times over! She's Latina, a sex worker, and I've got her back! I'm not going to play into some hierarchy of "traditionally educated" Latina versus "sex worker" Latina (because many sex workers have degrees, are more than just their job, kinda like you, and are intelligent business people).

Perhaps Laureano didn't intend to set up a "hierarchy of 'traditionally educated' Latina versus 'sex worker' Latina," but, to me, that's exactly what she did in her tweets and is doing in her blog post in a less-than-subtle way and, more importantly, before Rios wrote a single word. An unfortunate result of this is that Laureano becomes part of the crew dismissing Rios — perhaps not as virulently as others, but still taking part in it. I would be more understanding of Laureano's position if she reacted to Rios' hiring after Rios wrote information and/or advice that was questionable if not outright sketchy, but to cast aspersions — especially in a public forums like Twitter and a blog — on Rios' ability to give sex advice simply because she's not viewed as "qualified" (translation: degreed) and before she's had a chance to prove herself perpetuates educational privileging — and for a

Latina to do this to another Latina is a textbook case of kyri-archy*.

By emphasizing that Rios is a sex worker whose credentials deserve to be questioned, by linking to an organization of "professional" sex educators and sexologists whom Latina should have used (instead of the implicit end of the sentence "this undegreed sex worker"), telling Rios to "reach out" if she needs "guidance, support, mentorship, or a second opinion," the sexologist threw shade on the sex worker on the assumption that Rios was incapable of doing the job and that Laureano and her educated colleagues were entitled to that job over Rios — again, before Rios put fingers to a keyboard. Such an invitation suggests that Rios is a rank amateur who needs to someone "learned" to lead her on the "correct" sex-advice path. If I was in Rios' place, I'd be offended by what Laureano said instead of being willing to reach out her.

So, to check my reality, I ran the whole situation by my friend, Tony. He responded, "I think I would listen to a porn star. She just finished working so many hours fucking. This sexologist just studied it." With that, the "masses" have spoken.

As of this writing, Rios is still writing the column and hasn't reached out to Laureano. Nor has *Latina*.

* * *

Andrea (AJ) Plaid *writes about race and sex at the award-winning race-and-pop-culture blog Racialicious. Her work has been reprinted at* Penthouse, Colorlines, *and New American Media, and she has been quoted in* Washington Post *and* Chicago Tribune. *Andrea also owns an eco-friendly safer-sex kit company, Freak Kits.*

THERESA (TJ) LIGHTFOOT

So What if We Didn't Call it "Feminism"?!
Feminism and Indigenous people

Feminism and its mysticism of the capital — as opposed to the lower case — "F" always seemed so pretentious to me. It may be because of the well held myth that feminism is something that is only talked about in universities or is restricted to that era people see on TV in black and white and therefore deserves a capital F. If someone had told me things like "it is not confined to those spaces and "it is a philosophy not restricted to one political movement" then this type of examination might not seem so hard. Even though this is not what happened in my experience as a youth, I do believe that feminism has been alive outside of university in our Indigenous communities in occupied "North America" throughout history and it is something that is everywhere in our communities today.

What I have seen is that feminism within the university system seems so passive and theoretical. It was taught to us as an approach to the fields of human services or footnotes in history books. It makes it appear that feminism in life outside of these institutions is reserved for the select few middle- to upper-class non-Native women. It appears this way because when the so-called "big" discussions about feminism go on — equal pay, lack of access to childcare and women's reproductive rights, — these get all the attention. Indigenous women's fight for linguistic survival is not viewed as a fight for women's rights or equality, nor is Native women's fight to end violence against sex workers. These issues are treated as separate, or pushed under the umbrella of "Native issues", not something that feminism would be concerned about. This is also mirrored in the way that Aboriginal women's networks have to distinguish themselves from non-Native feminist organizations. This is because when it comes down to the subject, the non-Native feminist movements treat being Indigenous as an "add-on", as if it is not integral to the overall experience. It means that while mainstream feminist issues are prioritized by the movement, Native women get the typical "oh those are Native issues" response, or we hear things like, "colonialism and its hang ups are too vast and broad for our scope and thus don't warrant inclusion".

Mainstream feminism appears to be about individual women getting ahead or making patriarchy more tolerable, while... in an Indigenous context it is more about making things better for a collective group of people and taking on the system that is responsible for the roots of patriarchy in the first place.

Furthermore, academics make it appear passive, as if it is just something that happens in random protests or on the sidelines of women's shelters; however I don't believe this to be the case at all. I believe real feminism is not merely about arguing for better treatment or the ability to get ahead in the current system, it's about true equality and restoring balance. It is a fight for survival and changing the patriarchal system. It is in the everyday work and struggles that don't make headlines. For example, it's in the push for accessible housing, learning about traditional medicines, educating youth and the list goes on. I think that by limiting feminist practise as to what is taught in narrow, academic contexts leads young people to turn their noses up at the term. Consequently, it gets treated as if it is not relevant in our communities (Indigenous ones). It gets judged as something that is disconnected to some of the most important issues in our lives as Indigenous people, like survival. I believe because we as Indigenous people have been fighting for over 515 years of colonization and genocide, which means fighting just to live, that it makes it appear as if feminism has to take the back seat or that these issues are separated out from feminism just having to be about "women's issues". I think this may be due to the fact that mainstream feminism appears to be about individual women getting ahead or making patriarchy more tolerable, while if feminism exists in an Indigenous context it is more about making things better for a collective group of people and taking on the system that is responsible for the roots of patriarchy in the first place. However it is due to this distinction that I argue that the two things are so vitally intertwined that you can't separate them; they are in our lives every day.

Feminism is not only for non-Indigenous people; we have feminism in our lives as Indigenous people, it just is not always referred to as such. As stated above I do believe this is due to the dichotomy of trying to survive genocidal policy and colonization that pushed it to the side when it was there all along. Prior to contact it is well known that women held important positions within our many nations, were respected and considered powerful. We were respected because we are the creators of life; in many cultures most communities relied heavily on vegetables that were grown and harvested by women. Many women were important medicine people and they also held our traditional stories and kept our languages alive. Because of all these things and more our people have always had to have "feminism" as an important value in our societies. We also know that historically women have been warriors who fought side by side with men in several situations.

In the not so long ago "history" of our people, Native women and Native women's rights have been something that people knew about, but with different movements taking the credit people in power have forgotten about it. There were public legal battles fought for Indigenous women's rights, but for some reason this never gets mentioned in the list of what "feminism" looks like today. For example the Indian Act was a racist piece of legislation in Canada that had as its aim the eradication of Indigenous people, and specifically included provisions to target Native women. These provisions controlled who could or could not be considered Indigenous, and therefore decided how many generations could follow. The provisions ultimately attacked Indigenous women who chose to marry and have children with non-Native men and their descendants. This piece of legislation had many repercussions but its main purpose was essentially to legally wipe out Indigenous people in Canada.

This changed with Bill C-31 in the mid-1980s when an Indigenous lawyer named Sandra Lovelace Nicholas with the support of many other Indigenous women brought the Indian Act to court to try to fight for the survival of our next generations. This is something many of us are proud of, something that many of us are talking about in our everyday lives as it still affects us. Bill C-31, however, is not the exception of where feminism exists for Indigenous people. There are Indigenous women out there who are fighting the battle against linguicide (Tove Skutnabb-Kangus defines linguicide as, "the killing of languages without killing the speaker"[1]), women who are fighting for our rights to have babies in more traditional ways by midwives, women who are fighting for their traditional lands and rights. Our people talk about it all the time, but it is never mentioned as the "check out that feminist philosophy in action" because as I mentioned before, it gets "othered' and lumped into the category of "Native issues".

Because of this lack of labelling Indigenous struggles as feminist the concept of "feminism" can sound alienating. When I get into discussions with other Indigenous youth sometimes they get put off by it. What I end up getting is this look that says that I am treading on dangerous territory. I believe a lot of that comes from not discussing feminism in an Indigenous context as mentioned above. But when the similarities are put into an Indigenous context you see people become passionate and ready "to join the fight'". I think that because of the separation and isolation of Indigenous realities in the mainstream feminist movement, "feminism" presented alone as one term or one word seems irrelevant to many youth, especially outside of an academic institution.

I think that if we were to envision feminism, and by that I mean feminism in all its meanings of the word, its philosophies and underlying drives, as a sticky note, you can see it in plenty of everyday experiences/buildings/movements etc. At its essence it appears to be concerned about the survival of people, equality and respect. It is crucial to clarify here that this should not be confused with situations where women are purportedly put into positions of "power". Even though there is a woman's face on a policy or statement or movement it can still be male oriented/paternalistic in nature, and still more of the same. It's like what I see in Indian Act politics: how an Indigenous person on the Indian Act Band Council can push items that might not favour the best interest of the people but they choose to put it through anyway because it has the potential for some gain. Although this is not always the case, it does happen and it is a reflection of acting in a colonial way. Furthermore, when the system they are engaging in is set up by a colonial government and not in-line with their own traditional practises, it's problematic at best.

I am ultimately arguing that feminism exists outside of academia and that it is alive in Indigenous communities. We have always had feminism in our communities, but with colonization forcing us to focus our attention on survival, the term "feminism" has been pushed to the background. But even though the term has been pushed aside, my point is that the essence of feminism has always been there — so what if we never called it that?

* * *

Theresa (TJ) Lightfoot *is a Two-Spirit, Mi'kmaq youth whose family is from Elsipogtog First Nation and Nova Scotia. She has a background in psychology and Native studies. She currently lives in Makkovik, Nunatsiavut with her wife.*

ENDNOTES

[1] Skutnabb-Kangus, Tove (2000). Pg 311-318, 362-374. Linguistic Genocide in Education-or World Wide Diversity and Human Rights? Mahwah, New Jersey, London. Lawrence Erlbaum Associates.

Photo taken by Jessica Yee

After the Third Wave and Challenging Your Textbook-isms

TWO POEMS BY
D. COLE OSSANDON

Introduction

While agreeing and settling on an identity (individual and group) is an important aspect, and even may seem integral in aiding in the coalescing of a movement, the existence of inaccurate and misrepresenting classifications (which are prevalent in academia as well as women's rights groups) can lead to divisions and exclusions within the feminist community. For instance, the perpetuation of dividing feminists into "first wave," "second wave," "third wave," etc. This has created a disconnect between generations of women, as well as ignoring those who came before (e.g. Indigenous nations who have always held what is now called feminist ideals as a part of their culture) and in some cases marginalizing the efforts of those who come next. Another example is the division present between feminists of colour and white feminists, as well as hetero-centric feminists and LGBT feminists, where often classifications are made and lines are drawn thereby excluding any who don't fit into the prescribed parameters.

After the Third Wave

The women who ran with the wolves
now run from the next generation.
     Real or perceived,
     for all or for some,
     there's a gap in the road.

Does anyone count after the third wave?
     When it dissipates on the shore,
     does another follow,
     or is the sea now dormant?

Fight for the F words.
Authority doesn't want to hear me say, "Fuck."
Friends don't want to hear me say, "Feminism."

Challenging Your Textbook-isms

Learning your beliefs
through the mouths around you.
Burning to please your mentors.

Changing the meaning of "virgin territory" —
my footsteps were down before the road,
my words true before the page.

Knowing my rights.
Even if they're not the same as yours.
Warranting a search of suspect bodies.

Is there room between
your feminism and womanism
    for mixed skin,
    like mine?

Is there room beyond
your sexual liberation and free choice
    for mixed sex,
    like mine?

Is there room after
your -isms
    for mixed boundaries,
    like mine?

* * *

D. Cole Ossandon is a writer and multidisciplinary artist from Toronto & Guelph, ON. Her poetry has appeared in Matrix Magazine, The Incongruous Quarterly, *ditch, Books@Torontoist, and in the Inanna Publications anthology* Other Tongues: Mixed-Race Women Speak Out. *Her art has appeared in* Branch Magazine *and she currently writes for* Shameless Magazine *and* Canada Arts Connect.

ROBYN MAYNARD

Fuck the Glass Ceiling!

I'm going to start this off with an anecdote, but to me it encompasses so many broader issues of what the *hell* is going on with 'the status of women today'. For me, a fundamental lesson in the complexities intrinsic to feminism took place in 2006, in getting together with poor young moms from different backgrounds to create a publication called *Migrant or Local...We're Vocal*. This was a contract position at a grassroots community organization based in a largely immigrant neighbourhood in Montreal. The goal of the project was to work with 'marginalized'[1] (i.e. racialized, poor, Indigenous) young moms as a project of self-expression and to share resources. We were a small group, and the participants consisted of young and poor single moms who lived in the neighbourhood, who as racialized, of (im)migrant background, or Indigenous single moms, fit the 'marginalized' label specified according to the funders of this project. We got together weekly to discuss what people wanted to be writing, drawing, or photographing for this publication. It was decided fairly early on that they wanted it to be about real issues that these young moms

---

[1] Nearer the end of the piece you will find a critique on this term, and an explanation of why I use 'marginalized' in quotations.

were dealing with — if it was to be about 'resources' then people also wanted to discuss the difficulty in accessing them. The publication was based on frank conversations that different young moms had about their lives. Through the course of this, the actual forces and people that *cause* marginalization were discussed such as; racism, difficulty accessing affordable housing, the inadequacy of welfare, police harassment, discrimination in healt care faced by young parents of colour — to name a few.

In one section there were first-hand accounts by the women physical and sexual violence at the hands of police officers, another dealt with the inadequacy of their social housing while being surrounded by condominiums, and the impossibility of raising children on such low welfare rates. We put all of this in a section called "Young Moms Talk About Shit That Matters". There were also stories about the birth of children, about abortions, and substance use. This publication was done in D.I.Y. style which included cutting and pasting photos, printing out their words and gluing them onto the page along with pictures of their children, poetry that other women had submitted, and photocopying it all into a booklet, along with important resources in the neighbourhood for health, legal advice, information on safe sex, etc. The covers were pink, purple, or blue, and the front image of the first edition was of a mother and child.

When the first issue of the publication came out, the funders — a conglomerate of members of 'community' organizations and others deemed to have a stake in so-called 'marginalized youth' — were decidedly unhappy. As anyone who has worked in the community sector knows, those who get to be considered 'the community' is a contentious issue, and those who are deemed to deserve a stake in the futures of 'marginalized' populations, and who control how funding is to be distributed, are often those who are part of institutions responsible for marginalizing these same people. The funders consisted of neighborhood police officers[2],

---

[2] Though there is not time or space here to deal with this, it is a very serious problem that police officers are having a say in how funding is determined, and how to deal with 'marginalization' of youth and people of colour. Regardless of their personal intentions or attributes, systematically the abuse and profiling and over-prosecuting communities of colour is well-documented and indisputable, and at this historical epoch their very function exists as a generalized attack on most 'disadvantaged' communities.

the school boards and child protection, as well as some smaller grassroots community organizations working in and with directly affected communities.[3]

Immediately after the first edition was published, there were problems with the funders: the publication was 'too negative' about our society, not 'inspiring' enough. The possibility that perhaps there were important lessons in the very fact that people had lived such negative and alienating experiences as young, poor, migrant, Indigenous, and racialized, single parents, and that in fact this was as perhaps an accurate mirror of our society, was never questioned. Rather the *content* was seen as flawed, which was further seen as the fault of the participants, and by default, myself. One woman, an immigrant to this country, struggling to raise a child while on welfare, and dealing with institutional racism, referred to Canada as a "concrete jungle", a phrase which was frequently pounced upon by the funders as ungrateful. The statement "fuck the police", emblazoned on one of the pages, was deemed too inflammatory, though this section was nuanced and included several stories of women who had experienced sexual and physical violence at the hands of police officers. If bravely sharing these tales wasn't 'empowerment' in action, then what was? What followed however, was precisely the opposite of empowerment.

Born in 1987, I ever-so-slightly missed the moment of discovery in the phrase coined by INCITE! Women of Colour Against Violence that "the revolution will not be funded". However, if I can think of a perfect example of this in my own life so far, it's this experience, in which a table of nearly *all* middle-class white people yielding social and political capital, were somehow specifically mandated to represent the "interests of marginalized

---

[3] Many people working and running small community-based organizations that work directly with poor, racialized and immigrant populations in their neighbourhoods are far more critical of the systemic obstacles that are part of creating their circumstances in the first place. However existing amidst a continuous and systematized lack of stable funding and a reliance *on these same funders* makes it dangerous and difficult for them to speak their minds freely in bureaucratic situations such as these, for fear of losing funding for crucial community programming needed I their neighborhoods. That their small and crucial organizations exist in such precarity makes it unnecessary and innacurate to condemn their silence, as consent in the same way as say, the police.

youth". It teaches us something about our society that these same people controlling the funding for a project for marginalized youth to express themselves, were both shocked and appalled when young, majority racialized women, expressed a rage and 'lack of respect' towards the forces that actually *create* their marginalization; police harassment, landlords, condos encroaching on their public housing, doctors treating them like animals, and the impossibility of going absolutely anywhere with strollers due to lack of interest and funding by the city. The lengths to which hypocrisy can go stunned me then and continue to do so to this day. If silencing the voices of poor single moms in their *first* attempt at publishing their words and life stories is not marginalization, then what is?

You can imagine the rest of the story: the funders cut the funding entirely and wanted no association with the project. The women involved had varying reactions: embarrassment, sadness, surprise, and anger. Apparently, literally silencing and censoring women is the new empowerment? (This was clearly bunk. What was eventually empowering was when we said "fuck it" and decided to print the publication anyways, and indeed go on to create a second edition, bureaucrats be damned[4].)

Breaking down the buzz-words: 'empowerment', 'marginalization', 'exploitation'

This whole project of *Migrant or Local...We're Vocal* has, over the process of several years of reflection, made me reconsider what we even mean we talk about 'empowering marginalized people'. This language is often necessary to appeal to the funders of programming aimed at poor, racialized, indigenous and (im)migrant peoples, and these funders are most often government-based or controlled. For starters, what is this 'marginalization' anyways? We need to look at all of this in a bigger picture: what do we really *mean* when we say that women, and people of colour, Indigenous women, and migrants, are 'marginalized'? If we misunderstand 'marginalization', we are certain to misunderstand 'empowerment'. Can 'marginalization' be defeated merely with

---

[4] We did, in the end, find funding, from an amazing radical community organization that gave me this contact, *Head & Hands*, and indeed published two issues, both of which are still available in Montreal.

self-expression? How do you 'empower' someone for whom 'marginalization' means that they quite literally are struggling to have the basic resources needed to survive? And if those supposedly 'empowering' them are structurally part of the problem, where does this leave us? Understanding the forces behind the systematic impoverishment of women is crucial in trying to answer these questions.

Providing young poor women of colour funding for various means of self-expression is in and of itself in many ways, empowering — building self-confidence is a necessary struggle in communities that have been historically denigrated by Canadian mass culture and society. However, we need to look at all of this in a bigger picture. We need to look, now, at 'structural marginalization', or what I would rather call 'structural exploitation'. You may notice now that I am deviating from my introductory anecdote, and this because this kind of experience is, indeed, the tip of the fucking iceberg, when we talk about structural marginalization and women. By using the term structural I mean that which is by design, or intrinsic to the functioning of a particular system. 'By design' doesn't mean some 'evil mastermind' out to do things out of malice, (e.g. when conservatives say that those on the left are 'conspiracy theorists' I think that this is what they imagine we think is the root of all exploitation.)

Next, let's examine 'marginalization'. I've always felt wary about the community sector's use of the word 'marginalized populations', but didn't always understand why I felt it was so dubious. Now I do: 'exploitation' has always been a better term than 'marginalization', because where marginalization just means that people are pushed into, or exist already in, the margins of society, it doesn't explain how, or why. The process of marginalization isn't intrinsic to the meaning of the word, and 'margins' seem to pre-exist, as a natural location for people to inhabit in a society. It seems like something that just accidentally happens, and needs to be fixed by pulling people into some kind of imaginary 'centre', which I imagine is meant to be the middle class, or something to that effect. It is a watered down description of the extreme hardships and daily violence experienced by those living in extreme poverty and facing the harshest realities of racism in our society, and it also disguises the reasons for why it takes place. The government often puts aside money to target populations that they deem as 'marginalized' due to economic and racial factors, to have them participate in various creative projects. These projects are often based around the language of empowerment. To me it's important to note that though *Migrant or Local…We're Vocal* and other such projects are indeed often personally empowering, it's rarely noted that the reason that people are 'marginalized' in the first place has much to do with this same government that wishes to empower them. The ever-decreasing ability for the poor, racialized, and Indigenous to access the basic food and shelter needs that 'marginalize' people is not addressed, and 'marginalization' seems to be a phenomenon that just *is*. The word 'exploitation' is clearer. The *process of exploitation* is inside of this word, it contains, in its definition, the fact that somebody is being exploited *for the benefit* of somebody else; it is describing a *relationship*. And *this* makes it easier to understand what is meant in stating that the status of racialized, Indigenous, and immigrant women today is 'structural'.

If you look to world history, I think you will find that calculated greed has done far more damage to human society's than has sadism, or the desire to hurt people just for the sake of it. The destruction of people's lives and dignities through processes of exploitation has always served the purpose of enriching societal elite. An understanding of structural exploitation allows you to name names, and point fingers, at those who are exploiting you. When we talk about exploitation instead of marginalization it is easier to understand the forces that drive exploitation in the world today: colonization, racism, and capitalism. To me, it is this understanding that is one of the fundamental steps of empowerment, if we want empowerment to be about being able to live with dignity and self-determination. Indeed, the misuse of the term 'empowerment' in the community sector became clear to me when our funding was *taken away* at that exact moment that 'empowerment' began to mean, to these women, addressing the *nature* of their 'marginalization'. I'm going to go into some examples of what *I* mean by the structural exploitation of women, especially women who are NOT white, in and outside of Canada, for the interests of a privileged few.

Beyond salary equity & the glass ceiling debate — the problem is structural!

The thousands of missing and murdered Indigenous women across Canada, and the lack of media coverage of this, is not because the Canadian government *is malicious and does harm just for the sake of it*. This is not the point. Canada has *always* had a stake in the destruction of the self-determination of Indigenous people; the very attempts to annihilate culture, and take away dignity, are both historically, and currently linked to *colonization*, and therefore the theft of Indigenous territory. We can see how colonization has affected Indigenous women from the history of taking away women's power through the imposition of band councils, of forcing girls into residential schools, and also in the way that Canada perpetuates the massive rates of poverty of Indigenous populations in Canadian cities. This can also be seen in the rates of incarceration[5], nearly 75% of the female prison population in the prairie provinces — these things are not 'accidents' or residuals of an unfortunate history of 'cultural misunderstanding'. There is profit, and power at stake here, just as there always has been.

The first part of colonization and cultural and physical genocide happened so that these 'Canadian cities' that so many of us inhabit now could be built and connected by railways and roads. 'Canada' has been built now, but, the violence of its creation is not historical legacy. Colonization is *ongoing*, and this is because there is *still* a benefit for the Canadian government, and Canadian corporations, to perpetuate the cultural destruction, incarceration, and systematic under-protection of Indigenous women. Trying to destroy Indigenous cultures' ability to survive helps Canadian financial interests because those very interests are still encroaching on Indigenous territory! Our mainstream media is successful in blacking out the continual theft of territory for profit. The Canadian extractive industry, logging companies, and hydroelectric dams are continually being imposed on indigenous communities, in Barriere Lake, the Matawa First Nations in Ontario, and more than can be named here.[6] The so-

---

[5] The Canadian prison budget exemplifies this perfectly, having been nearly *doubled* in the last five years.

[6] www.miningwatch.ca has comprehensive information about mining on Indigenous territories.

called 'Oka Crisis' was *not* the only time that First Nations people have had to face theft of their land in recent history; the media has merely changed its coverage. As we know it is women who bear a large burden of impoverishment and displacement, and because of this colonization is *always* a feminist issue.

What is another example of how oppression of women and people of colour is structural? We hear occasionally in the news about the 'feminization of poverty'. World leaders of so-called first world nations publicly treat poverty in the global south as a 'sad' thing that they want to help, not as the outcome of a deliberate economic strategy that they purposefully exacerbate for profit. And again, I say not as a deliberate strategy because it's not as if they are meanies who want to hurt people, but because, in reality, this is what is occurring: they are systematically stripping the majority world of its resources to enrich themselves and the large corporations they are accountable to. This isn't new, it was much more explicit in the days of world colonization proper, when sections of land, resources, and people were literally just taken, to make profit for European nations.

The settler colonies now continue this through a different language of corporate driven, government-based economic trade policies, using programs like the International Monetary Fund, and the World Bank. The Canadian government has a huge stake in a global economy in which rich nations literally coerce poor nations, the former colonies, into sacrificing the large majority of their natural resources. This is done either with threat of actual violence, as Canada recently supported in the coup d'état in Haiti, (a land which has barely any natural resources left to be stolen at this point), or with threat of starvation and further impoverishment through threatened trade embargos.

We talk about Canada, the United States, etc., as 'idea economies' but it's hard to ignore that we still use things to survive, things which are made, sewed, grown, picked, soldered, by *people*. Some of these things we need, like food, but most of them our 'idea economies' become rich by selling things made of plastic to each other with resources that came from *somewhere*, and were built by *somebody* who did *not* become rich through building it. Our fruit does not magically appear on our plate because people in our society are somehow instantaneously 'intelligent'. There are strawberry farms outside of Montreal made up of all migrant women, who are literally locked into their sleeping places at night, and shipped back to their countries of origin for the off-season with no chance of ever living here legally. Abroad there are countless factories in the global south filled with women being paid approximately $1 a day in making the textiles that people in Canada wear on their day to the office in their 'idea economy'. Non-status women work in terrible conditions in sweat-shops *in Canada*, because they can be threatened with deportation if they quit. Filipino women work in 'live-in caregiver' programs where they are often denied wages,

These different kinds of 'marginalized women' are not all arbitrary and disconnected forms of people falling through the cracks at home or abroad — these are pillars of the global economy.

abused on the job, forced into overtime, and fired for being pregnant, because according to the law they are under threat of deportation if they choose to change employers due to poor working conditions.

When you get down to it, the point that I'm trying to make is that these different kinds of 'marginalized women' are not all arbitrary and disconnected forms of people falling through the cracks at home or abroad — these are pillars of the global economy. These are issues of labour, and of the global economic system. By this I mean the basic idea of where our *things* come from: how they are made, and by whom, how they get here, and who profits from them. This is, has always been and always will be a feminist issue, because women — and by women I mean migrant women, racialized women, women in the global south, Indigenous women — bear the massive brunt of this. Continuing plans of government fiscal austerity make it so that women living on welfare are becoming more and more vulnerable, and social housing is less and less accessible, though military and prison budgets continue to rise dramatically. This is violence towards women, straight up — and it's not incidental, but fundamental, to the world that we live in today. So when we talk about the 'feminization of poverty', it is simply incorrect to frame it as an abstract phenomenon of women who Canada would help if it could.

The reason I'm focusing so much on the fact that there are people benefitting from perpetuating the dire situation faced by women in Canada and worldwide is first to dispel the notion that not holding racist and sexist stereotypes is proof of having eliminated racism and having achieved gender equality. Or that in closing the gaps of 'salary equity' between women and men in positions of power, that we have 'solved' sexism. Most importantly, it is because of the extreme need we have to point fingers where they need to be pointed. We need to hold the government, financial institutions, national and international corporations *accountable* for their role in the daily injustice and violence faced by women.

Just as important, and this ties back to my introductory anecdote, it's not only the leaders of financial institutions, weapons companies, mining companies, and government officials, who hold responsibility here. We also need to challenge the power distribution of in our local communities and in our cities. This situation that we live in, in which 3% of the world holds nearly the entirety of its wealth and the poverty of women, especially racialized, migrant, and Indigenous women in the so-called 'first world' nations, could not possibly be accomplished and held in place without the lower down bureaucrats. We don't only see this on the global level but across the board, and this is why my experience with *Migrant or Local…We're Vocal!* was so powerful to me. What I'm saying is that we need to call a spade a spade when so-called 'community' voices sell out and water down politics of oppression so as to not rock the boat, to keep people from demanding change where it so often begins: at the grassroots level. My anecdote at the beginning of this piece was to demonstrate exactly this point: we need to stop believing in the supposed 'benevolence' of *anyone* who tries to deal with 'marginalized people' through an abstract kind of empowerment, without any comprehension, or indeed with a *refusal to examine*, what it would actually take to have justice. People make careers off of sitting around different tables supposedly dealing with issues of 'youth marginalization', 'women's marginalization', seeing them as disconnected, yet important 'issues' without ever tangibly taking on the root causes of why there is, indeed, exploitation.

What I learned through the process of helping create and fight for *Migrant or Local…We're Vocal!* is that when push comes to shove, people in these positions are often more willing to defend the very same status quo that they are, on paper, helping people to fight. I witnessed one occasion where funders, who supposedly exist for the purpose of 'empowering the marginalized', were forced to lay their cards on the table in terms of where their loyalties lie, and more often than not it was *not with* the people who are actually 'marginalized'[7].

Towards justice

The statement 'another world is possible' is the force that drives so many of us, but there are steps that it takes to *build* this world — it cannot be built off the backs of the exploited labour of our sisters. I strongly believe that local, grassroots, and community-based justice movements have the biggest potential to be truly effective, and therefore cannot be controlled by bureaucrats, be they higher ups or lowers down.

Justice means — justice *has* to mean — an end to people deliberately destroying generations of cultures, of women, of lives, and of dignity, for personal political and economic gain. It has to mean an end to turning a blind eye to oppression this for professional status and for fear of rocking the boat. It's more than 'know your enemy', it's knowing how, and for what reason, they are your enemy. This is why those who desire to maintain the status quo do not want 'empowerment' to include digging too deep, or to result in anger. This

> Justice means — justice *has* to mean — an end to people deliberately destroying generations of cultures, of women, of lives, and of dignity, for personal political and economic gain.

anger *should* be frightening to those making the most from this situation. Of course we shouldn't expect the ones profiting from the system in which we currently live to let anybody say that on their dime, their 'empowerment' has crucial limits. Knowledge, empowerment, and justice are scary concepts to those that uphold and benefit from the status quo in societies that whose economies are based on colonization, racism, and exploitation of the poor. This is because they can effectively take away the *material* aspects of our power, they can try to destroy the cultural

---

[7] Again here I find it important to emphasize my earlier point that small grassroots organizations working directly in communities should not be ethically condemned in the same manner due to the fact that their very survival is often determined by their deference to state interests.

aspects of our power, but 'people power' is and has always been a real, tangible, force in society, regardless. Building tangible movements based around the basic right of people to live with dignity is possible. Doing so without the permission and funding of state funding is necessary. People power is terrifying to those who have systematically stripped people of their means of survival for generation after generation, building condos and mansions off of the 'misfortune' — read 'armed or unarmed robbery' — of an ever-expanding poor, at home and abroad.

The real point I'm trying to get across, in writing this piece, is that fighting for 'women's issues' does not exist in a vacuum — there are forces at work here that *put* women in the different situations that we find ourselves in. Because of this fact, it follows that there ARE real solutions, but they're not always easy. *Real* empowerment of women, of 'marginalized people' is scary because what it is what it sounds like. It involves things like popular education, mass civil disobedience, and refusing to accept the moral authority of illegitimate power structures. Knowledge and *real* empowerment are threats to the status-quo, and they shouldn't be watered down, they should be taken as such. Gender equality will *not* be achieved by having more female CEO's! Fuck fighting to get past the glass ceiling: *it's on*, and there should be no mincing words about it. Fight the power.

* * *

Robyn Maynard *is a community organizer, writer and musician living in Montreal. She co-hosts No One Is Illegal Radio, and is part of grassroots movements for migrant justice, and against racial profiling and police violence.*

CASSANDRA POLYZOU

Feminism and Eating Disorders
Wishful thinking for a more caring attitude

I have listened to many feminist scholars and activists talk about positive body image and the ridiculous and damaging representations of women and men in the media, and as a young feminist I quickly recognized the importance of valuing a range of body types. The negative impacts of objectifying bodies in the media and patriarchal beauty standards have been discussed over and over again by feminists, and I, like most feminists, was once very secure in my understanding of feminism as a safe space for all bodies. However, that position shifted when I realized I was suffering from an eating disorder.

To me, the notion of being a feminist with an eating disorder seemed contradictory, causing me to have a great deal of self doubt. It took me three years since fully recognizing my disorder to be able to consider myself a feminist again and to stop expecting the feminist "police" to call me out as a fake. Today I can honestly say that my personal experiences in the treatment of my disorder within the organizations and practices of eating disorder counselors and support workers, have taught me more about my own feminism than any women's studies course I attended or Judith Butler text I have read. I also learned a great deal about the "outside" of feminism, the places where young women and men, cis- and trans-gendered, live and exist in the blindside of feminist theory and practice. A question I asked myself over and over again as I went through treatment years ago and listened to young people's countless painful stories of their anorexia and bulimia nervosa, was "Where is feminism for these people?" Where is feminism when more and more young people develop eating disorders? Why are the lessons about positive body image and the false objectification of bodies not enough?

Eating disorders are said to be strongly related to a person's social position. Gender, class, race, and physical and mental states are among the factors in the development of eating disorders, but with more women experiencing eating disorders than men, gender is an especially relevant factor. There needs to be a lot more discussion on how cis-sexism and heteronormativity are not taken up in most discussions on eating disorder prevention in the first place. Behaviours like dieting, negative self-judgment, and obsessing over being thin are reinforced and adversely impacted by gender inequity and so-called "gender norms". Feminism definitely has a role to play in addressing eating disorders, but in this chapter I suggest some problems with how feminists take up eating disorders, as well as some ideas for what feminists could be doing to help individuals experiencing eating disorder symptoms.

As I quickly searched for articles that mention feminism, or feminist principles, I was not surprised to see that there is limited mention of feminism in eating disorder journals. Likewise, not very much is being written about eating disorders in feminist journals. I did notice some feminists calling on prevention programs and eating disorder clinics to incorporate a feminist analysis of the impact of gender on self and body experiences. Feminists want these institutions to recognize gender as a high level risk factor. While feminism may be calling on eating disorder programs and service providers to emphasize the impact of gender inequity and the oppression of women in society, research shows that individual differences, personality traits, and family variables strongly impact how a person reacts to sociocultural pressures and standards. Feminists, as far as I've experienced, are looking to criticize and point out the cultural sources of eating disorders and to me that has not helped combat eating disorders one bit.

As a feminist scholar-activist, I have a deep understanding of the gender imbalance in our society, but that understanding and even my experience as an engaged, do-it-yourself, grassroots activist did not help me recover from my eating disorder. I believe feminism can be a great analytical tool, but blaming eating disorders on a consumerist Western cultural ideal, or our patriarchal society, does not readily provide strategic tools for people to overcome or avoid eating disorders. The reality of anorexia or bulimia nervosa is that they are related to both socio-cultural and individual circumstances, including mental health, and subconscious processes like the internalization of social standards, low-self esteem, perfectionism, etc. When talking about eating disorders, feminists need to acknowledge the individual, the internal processes that affect a person's eating disorder, and the importance of supporting a person's unique path to recovery if they choose it. If feminists restrict the discussion regarding eating disorders to "bigger picture" ideas and concepts like gender inequity, or cultural oppression they are more likely to alienate the person who is dealing with very micro-level, real, and personal symptoms. Emphasizing that women, cis- and trans-, are frequently exposed to harassment or that they experience greater body image pressures than men, or that it is the fault of Western cultural values that pressures girls/boys to be thin does not necessarily give a person trying to recover from an eating disorder any tools to cope or break the habits that control their life. No, instead she might be thinking about how worthless she is, how out-of-control her life is and maybe how controlling food and her body are the only things she can get a handle on. Ideas, theories, and cultural analysis all exist in the intellectual and cerebral realm, but the things this girl is thinking are a mix of emotions and often distorted thoughts. So what if the Western stereotypical standard for beauty is unattainable and caused by patriarchal values? Pointing this out might not

Feminism can be a great analytical tool, but blaming eating disorders on a consumerist Western cultural ideal, or our patriarchal society, does not readily provide strategic tools for people to overcome or avoid eating disorders.

have a strong or lasting effect on someone with, or soon to have, an eating disorder because it boils down to an idea and ideas can be overcome by other threads of reasoning or emotional responses. So while talking about gender inequity or cultural values in the context of eating disorder prevention is important, I believe feminists need to explore and speak to the personal and deep psychological impacts of eating disorders. It also wouldn't hurt to ask people who experience eating disorders for their input.

If we look into the causes of eating disorders, we see a unique picture drawn for each individual. Every person has a different background, different pressures, different emotional and psychological landscapes, and different socio-economic privilege that contribute to the causes of their eating disorder. It is never as straight forward as "I want to be thin." The development of an eating disorder is not as simple as seeing a beautiful, airbrushed, thin, white, able-bodied model on the cover of some magazine and deciding to starve yourself in order to emulate her image. Nor, is it as simple as saying all individuals with eating disorders experience the same causes or pressures. Some people can develop eating disorder behaviours to cope with trauma, abuse, stress, lack of control over their lives, low self-esteem and self-worth, and the list goes on. There are also family situations and dynamics that can increase or decrease the risk of someone developing an eating disorder.

Treating every person as a unique individual can help make feminism more relevant to the women experiencing and at risk of developing eating disorders. Instead of turning to the counselors, public health workers, and service providers who are the front-line workers against eating disorders, feminists need to look at what a person with an eating disorder needs in order to cope in society. There is always room for improvement in treatment and prevention, I do not deny that, but instead of being the eternal criticizer of mainstream institutions, feminists can take up space at the table to affect individual lives. How? By becoming active participants in the battle against eating disorders in classrooms, in activist circles, and in community building. Another way to address this is by breaking down the notion that all women are fundamentally alike as they march under the banner of womanhood. In the same way that feminism and the notion of a universalized womanhood have been critically examined as representing a white dominated Western perspective, the notion that all women have the same psychological and mental make-up needs to be taken apart. All women, cis-and trans-gendered, are not alike and in the case of eating disorders, not all are wired the same way, meaning that every person's relationship to their own body, to food, to family, and to stress is necessarily different. We also shouldn't depend on doctors to let us know if someone in our community is suffering, we should try to make our communities safer and comfortable spaces for people to share their vulnerabilities and their uniqueness.

Most importantly, I wish activists who understand how oppressive attitudes — such as racism, sexism, ableism, and the like — can be injurious, would take on a more caring and supportive attitude towards eating disorders and negative body image. People with an eating disorder can sometimes struggle with managing the realities of them for their entire lives, at times relapsing and at the worst of times losing themselves in it entirely. If we understand the severity of the disorder than there is a chance we will stop treating it like a joke. I believe the way feminism and women's studies have handled the objectification of bodies in the media and the Western cultural obsession with thin bodies make eating disorders out to be simply manifestations of these oppressive norms. Eating disorders are not abstract 'concepts', they are real. Eating disorders are often presented by women's studies or feminists as part of an unhealthy and oppressive Western culture, and people who experience eating disorders are framed as either victims, or willful participants. Moreover, people with eating disorders can be hated and disrespected in the name of the noble fight against misogyny because they can be included on the same 'team' as the oppressors. To be clear, not every feminist I know hates on anorexics, but I have lost count of the times I have heard disrespectful comments made about skinny women, or about people who restrict their food, or jokes about pretty women puking up their dinner. Not that all skinny women have an eating disorder, but I think the negative sentiment towards people who fit the unrealistic Western beauty standard also reflects a negative attitude towards people who experience eating disorders or who struggle with the desire to look like the ideal body.

Feminists need to be sensitive to how they treat people with eating disorders, recognizing that eating disorders are not self-inflicted and addressing the destructive tendency of 'blaming the victim'. In my experience, many individuals who have eating disorders are extremely intelligent and tend to be perfectionists, or at least have very high expectations of themselves. Some of the most outstanding, opinionated, dynamic, and strong women I have ever met, I met while I was in treatment. Yet, when I consider the shame and stigma associated with eating disorders I realize that there is a perception that people who have eating disorders are weak. The stigma around eating disorders implies that a person is weak if they 'give in' to the Western cultural pressures to be thin and they should be deeply ashamed that they have put themselves in the position they are in. The concept of 'blaming the victim' is deeply engrained in some social movements and in mainstream society, reinforcing the often already present self-hatred that some eating disorder sufferers experience.

Learning to accept yourself, what makes you different from everyone else, and your own faults is an important part of eating disorder recovery. The struggle to be perfect and the increasing demand to be successful in every way (ie. career, school, family, sexuality, body, etc.) play huge roles in the mentality that leads someone to sacrifice their well-being in order to fit the ideal. As feminists look to make their communities stronger and to support individuals, they should look at the demands that are placed on activists and community organizers. The average activist is trying to be an entirely ethical consumer, on-call for the moment when a quick rebuke is needed to a racist, sexist, ableist, classist, or transphobic comment is made, while also attending to the demands of school, work, family, relationships, a community garden project, cycling advocacy, and more. At this point, it is important for me to state that I do not mean to complain about these choices or the amount of work that each of them requires. However, I think it is important to recognize that these choices are difficult and have an emotional and psychological impact on activists. To understand the world as made up of unique and diverse individuals, also means making space for different levels of commitment to various activities, including those that we hold dear as social justice activists. It means cutting others and ourselves some slack when judging each other, or when observing something that makes us uncomfortable. Concepts and ideals are important building blocks, but they do not, alone, make healthy people.

I would wish for is a kinder feminism. One that considers each individuals as unique, flawed, and beautiful, and takes a step out of the classroom and non-profit organization and into every person's life.

* * *

Cassandra Polyzou *lives in Waterloo, Ontario with her husband, and her canine and feline companions. She has worked in the not-for-profit industry for close to ten years. Cassandra has a Master's in Cultural Analysis and Social Theory from Wilfrid Laurier University, with a focus on cross-cultural/transnational feminist collaboration.*

REFERENCES

Piran, Niva. 2010. "A Feminist Perspective on Risk Factor Research and on the Prevention of Eating Disorders", *Eating Disorders*, 18:3, 183 - 198.

Tiggerman, Marika., and Stevens, Claire. 1999. "Weight Concern Across the Life-span: Relationship to self-esteem and feminist identity." *International Journal of Eating Disorders*. 26:1, 103-106.

My Secret

A POEM BY PEGGY COOKE

I have a secret
I never read any Virginia Woolf
Any bell hooks, any Betty Friedan
I don't know any theory

I am a white lady
With every privilege you can name
When people see my skin colour, hear me talk
They must think I am a product
Of Women's Studies
But I have a secret

I sit in feminist meetings
Discussion groups, fundraisers
I don't have a clue what
This lady's talking about
That lady's talking about
All nice white ladies
All like me

But I know what I've seen
What I've lived
I knew privilege, intersectionality, silencing
Before I knew the terms
I know when I am a bad ally
Even when I can't name what I did wrong

I stood on a rooftop
Hand in hand with a Dominican boy
I loved
We looked out over the Free Trade Zone
And I knew then, at 17
What those smokestacks meant
For his future and for mine
I knew then about privilege
About my white skin, the place of my birth
The million lucky coincidences that made me able
To turn around and leave
And made the opposite true for him

I knew then, and struggle now
And nothing those classes, theories, scholars could say
Could make it any easier, or any more difficult
To walk the line
Between ally
And benevolent oppressor

Feminism is not my major
It is my story

* * *

Peggy Cooke *is the volunteer co-ordinator at the Fredericton Morgentaler Clinic in New Brunswick and a media representative for the Abortion Rights Coalition of Canada. She is a 26-year-old feminist activist, and a bisexual fat white woman with a BPhil in Interdisciplinary Leadership. She is a founding member of the NB Rebelles Gumboot Troupe which uses gumboot dancing to deliver an anti-oppression message.*

DIANDRA JURKIC-WALLS

Mistakes I Didn't Know I was Making

Or "A portrait of a feminist as a young academic", or even, "Battlestar Academica": A short essay about my time at grad school where I was trained to come up with long witty titles for my writing (among other things)

I willingly admit that despite all of the trappings of my life that are beyond "normal" or rooted in a first-generation "Canadian", working-class, inner-"city", FAT girl's upbringing, I lust after heteronormative, white, upper-middle class America television programming. I lust after the girls. With their flowy willow-toned or brassy-blonde locks piled high or long on top of their "don't cha wish your girlfriend was hot like me" bodies, these girls inspire a semi-charmed life that I desire. They have lives that I never had, nor ever will have, and the yearning, well, that's just what American woman-hating capitalism ordered: I can't be happy with myself, so I have to just WISH I could be like one of them.

And when it comes to life-subjects like university, sometimes I have wished I could be them. Take for example the life of Miss Rory Gilmore (of *Gilmore Girls*' fame). Sure Rory had a hard knock life, child of a single mother who grew up in a shack outside of a fancy Connecticut Inn. Her character exists solely to not only have all of those things her mother sacrificed in order to raise her only daughter, but also those things that her grandparents offered her mom, but her mom refused. Like Blair Waldorf of *Gossip Girl*, Yale is the only school of choice for any respectable Gilmore offspring. And like characters from *Gossip Girl*, a Gilmore having the option of Yale isn't a choice of affordability, eligibility, or access but of sheer want and hope for receiving.

But, that's enough about these upper-middle class characters who present as having access to it all. The reason I'm dragging you through my prime-time-girls-who-wear-tights-and-corduroy-skirts rant is to point out that television meant for American teen audiences (which I have obviously gobbled up) can really screw a girl up! I was not bred to attend university and was actually the first person in my entire family to even go to university, but I'm supposed to believe, from these shows, that it's my destiny to attend and more importantly that I have ready and easy access because I'm white.

My experience on campus, both in and out of class, was based on my assumption that I could discuss and demonstrate my own world view as something valid, or even relevant to the discussion/learning at hand. HA!

And, I did have access. I was socialized by my parents and the school system to go to university because it was the only way I would "get a good job" and achieve my rightful place in the "middle-class" (ha!). It was presented as my only option. From what I can remember it also had something to do with "not getting pregnant before I graduated high school" (something my mom, who got pregnant with me before she graduated, said I would benefit from...not getting pregnant, that is). I didn't really want to go to university and while I felt like I mastered high school, I took only the bare minimum that I needed to graduate and had to slag my way through two years of community college to gather enough transfer credits to get into a bonafied university.

When I did get to a university to work on an actual degree, I felt like I spent much of my time in conflict with what I was being taught (and how it was being taught to me). I didn't understand how I was supposed to fit in, or even if I should. My experience on campus, both in and out of class, was based on my assumption that I could discuss and demonstrate my own world view as something valid, or even relevant to the discussion/learning at hand. HA! It was/is through my conflict with school and the things I was "taught" that helped me define who I was as a feminist, especially because it gave me something to define myself against.

At university I realized there was this whole other world that dedicated itself to feminism, anti-oppression work, and gender studies without actually accomplishing anything tangible or "for the people". You could take classes where you studied resistance, rather than simply resist. I was confounded! What was feminism without action? An upper division class on Utopias? Or an introduction class geared towards straight-out-of-high school teeny boppers who "know nothing" of the oppression of women, so are taught about emancipation and the history of the women's movement (when, really, high schoolers could teach everyone a thing or two about oppression)?

Full disclosure: I majored in Canadian History because I'm obsessed with the motives behind colonization, and I still don't understand how money and wanderlust can justify such a terrible thing. I did, however, take two Women's Studies classes. I was very confused taking these classes and didn't understand (and still don't) why we take a class on how we're oppressed to learn about our oppression? (Even though this is probably true for some people). And more often then not, my feminisms and experiences being oppressed and oppressing others didn't fit into the model of how oppression was taught (that oppression was something that happened to "other" people, that's why we were studying them it in books). Having seen that feminism was being taught and defined as something untouchable and obviously not created by youth or radicals, I began to seek out community-based activists and more ways to express my activism and feminist politic that were beyond arguing about date rape in a classroom and actually engaging with the issue on campus and in the community.

When I decided to go to graduate school to study capital "F" feminism (eg. feminism in books and the study of how feminism [dis]functioned) I really only had two Women's Studies classes under my belt, but had already spent the previous 10 years (I was 24) volunteering in a variety of capacities for feminist organizations, and dodging bullets in my classes/community/high school for my "radical" beliefs that gay people deserve parades, women shouldn't be beaten up by their spouses or strangers, and that young girls shouldn't be dominated by the beauty industry or encouraged to hate themselves. I thought that all activists, all young women, and all feminists held these ideas, but what I didn't realize until graduate school was how differently these beliefs could be applied...or not applied at all.

Now, before I open the flood gates and summarize my walk in the sun at university (True Blood style), I want to preface with a few starter points:

1. I've set up my reaction and response in list format as a way to help me put concrete definition/language behind my experiences. As mentioned above, I am still dealing with confusion as to where everything meets (or doesn't) and what it all means to me; using lists helps me keep my focus and lets me get out my stream of consciousness while hopefully still making sense.
2. I am not setting myself up as a martyr. I did not go in to slay the dragon for the sake of my feminist generation to get slayed right back by another generation. I have not "taken one for the team" and I'm not using this essay to make anyone think that I should be felt sorry for.
3. I don't regret going to graduate school, but I'm sure I could've done something more constructive with my time and brain.
4. The "Academy" hates kids (and feminists).

***

I went to grad school because I wanted to study the historical legacy of young feminists in Canada. But at the time I started school there were maybe two or three texts written by young Canadian feminists and they hadn't been covered enough or even recognized enough for me to write about their impact (the documents, not the feminists). One thing led to another as it tends to do in graduate school in the arts and I changed my focus: I was going to put together a true third-wave feminist text and submit it to the Academy to challenge "the man" to move over, change its ways, and let the little grrrls in.

I chose third-wave feminism because I feel/felt it is/was a kind of feminism I identify with. Third-wave feminism is a "wave" of feminism that intends to encompass Generation-X feminists and younger feminists. The definition was given to itself by a young feminist in the 1990s and much of academic and dominant discourse about young feminists has revolved around "third-wave". So, I set out to put together a massive zine that was composed of a handful of essays I wrote about myself (a feminist) and third-wave feminism. I made drawings, I wrote in code, and I cut out pictures of porn stars, hollywood starlets, and housewives to paste in the margins (haha, get it? margins?).

I was really lucky that I chose a small university and had access to some of the most inspiring and encouraging feminist professors and mentors...ever! This mish-mash of feminists pushed me to be more academic and consider as many facets of my project as possible. They also opened their minds and let me challenge them with my new zany feminisms. When it came time for me to defend my thesis to the Academy (a process by which students present their work to professors and other students and a small committee decides your fate) my committee and I concurred that "not all academic feminists" must be against young feminists, because as my experience proved, I was welcomed, encouraged, and supported by a handful of Gen X and Boomer Feminists.

Some of my fellow students, too, were (and are) incredible feminists, activists, and friends. The fact that my defence was packed with people from all over my life in Prince George says a lot: we had community, a common understanding, and wanted to work for the same things. Like most people who face a thesis defence, my defence was a culmination of my experiences and education, my attempt to put my work forth, hold my breath, cross my fingers, and actually HOPE that "the man"/"the Academy" says YES, OK, "I get it". It was also terrifying as hell.

Even though I passed my defence, I feel like the changes I was asked to make to my final copy, and the manner in which they were requested somehow re-traumatized me to remember all the non-cool things that happened while I was in grad school. I remembered all the bullshit I had to go through like, the jerking around (like not being allowed to use my transit pass or my library privileges because I couldn't afford to pay my tuition, but having to pay those fees regardless, after the semester was over, because I had signed up for a two year plus program), and the hate-on for feminists (such as profs who openly told other students that what I was studying wasn't "real" academia because it was women's studies, or exercising the desire for more "open learning" and being told we weren't allowed to organize our presentation in a "circle" at a graduate conference, or profs in classes telling me, in front of other students, that my "gender studies" or "feminist" view point wasn't as valid as their X, Y, and Z viewpoint). My general approach went something like this: "this is me, I'm a kid, I'm a feminist, I'm an activist, this is the third wave, I identify as third wave...hey there, "man", can you accept me on my terms?" And the obvious answer is no.

I'm not going to deny that the work I submitted or did at the university wasn't the best work anyone in the world could do (because there's always someone out there who does it better), but it was the best work I could do and I was/am open to learning, changing, and adapting. What I felt like happened, though, was that the complications with my work and my approach outweighed the positive effect on "the man" and I really had no effect on "the man" at all. In fact, with all the bullshit that happened during grad school, the whole process of putting my thesis out there as an attempt at reflecting myself and feminism and having to amend it into something unrecognizable just so I could pass, graduate, is a starting place in proving my point: radical feminists aren't welcome, young people aren't welcome, and our voice, our experience, and our approach isn't welcome, desired, wanted, or even recognized as a positive adjective contribution.

***

Okay, so I know that in the end I passed, and I made great friends, and my work had an impact and the community had an impact on me. I even developed positive relationships with academics, but I still don't consider my time at grad school a success. On the same note, the issues I had with grad school, "the man", and feminism in the Academy, the things that I consider the "un-successes", are definitely where I would point out what has gone sour (or as always sour?) in Women's Studies, and even why feminists just need to say no to going to university and becoming academic feminists.

1. No matter how long it's been around, Women's Studies (and any other department that studies oppression) is continuously isolated and ghettoized in the Academy: meaning funding is repeatedly reduced, feminist methods are discounted as feminist and then amalgamated by every other department, and class content and campus response always hinges on the dominant response, "but where is the MEN'S centre?". Also, our department had very little working-scholarship opportunities, there was really only one scholarship for all Women's Studies students at the university, and other departments didn't consider us Gender Studies students as "real" academics when we were floating or teaching in other departments. But still, Women's Studies departments keep trying to win the favour of their institutions and even the broader Canadian public. Remember the whole kerfuffle in the Spring of 2010 when someone in the *National Post* wrote an editorial that Women's Studies was dead/unneeded and the academic feminist world organized a response? Of course Women's Studies is alienating to young men in the introduction to why you're oppressed by your boyfriend classes! Who cares? Girls are alienated by their gross sexist teachers in whatever other department they're in! That didn't make a national debate on CBC's radio show, *The Current*. The general Canadian Media Mindset doesn't care about Women's Studies so is it even necessary to have a broad "F"eminist response?

2. You cannot be a young feminist activist AND an academic. It's the ultimate oxymoron. Case in point: I used words like "our" and "us" or even "you" because I wanted my zine-thesis to be a rallying cry for young feminists who also felt alienated by "the man" and hated the idea of grad school and hated the overarching patriarchy and wanted to change something. When I went to defence I was asked to take all of these out. I had to make my thesis more nuanced and less alienating of others, I was told by using words like "our" and "us" I was assuming that all feminists were the same and was being oppressive in my lumping all of "us" together with "my feminism" or the "movement". Even my use of words like "the fight" and "the man" became questionable: how could I say that I was trying to subvert and challenge the dominant patriarchy and then also rely on grouping feminists together to find an agreement on something so that we could rally against and be political and radical in the face of massive patriarchy? Well, the answer was that I couldn't.

And it's complicated. It would be an obvious move for me as a white person to say that my oppression is the same as your oppression (whoever you are), that we experience the same pressure under "the man". It's been an obvious move by white feminists for decades. But, I know this is bullshit, because I am obviously responsible towards some of the oppression towards you. It would also be very privileged of me to say, "we're all oppressing each other," because you may experience more oppression than I could imagine in my lifetime.

What I find the hard part is, and this is what I sought to find out post-defence from those with the criticism, is to determine what words I would use to describe my want to join forces with you (or you with me) to somehow stand up to shared oppressors (because I think we can all admit we're under a global patriarchy fuck), but at the same time avoid alienating you and amass your experience at the same time. In theory, this is something that capital "F" and academic feminism hasn't achieved. I think that this has definitely been achieved on a personal level in my own life and I am so grateful for those opportunities and experiences, but in an academic setting I found it frustrating and impossible: How am I supposed to inspire you to do blank and how are you supposed to inspire me to do blank if it's all about our individual struggle because we're tippy toeing around language because we're afraid to be labelled a racist? What are our other words for commonality (even if our only commonality is resisting)?

Even though I often don't want to strike up commonality with "white folk" or "the white way" of academia, I felt like my successful personal relationships that have showed me that I can have solidarity with you (whoever you are) weren't given the space to be theorized or even the space to be mis-stepped and thrown together in a confusing stream-of-consciousness fashion (much like right here). I was reminded that I was getting a Master's Degree. So I just had to suck it up and make my thesis a document that reflected what I needed to do to get a Master's Degree. Good-bye resistance!

3. It's really hard to be a kid and go to grad school. It's not the kind of environment where I could speak my language. I often felt that I was the odd one out and pressured to be a "professional" and speak like an adult. Sure, I was in grad school so there was a sense of decorum, like I couldn't really wear jeans to my defence could I? (so what was I thinking? that my potty mouth was OK? um, well, yes?) But, being a kid in a pool of boomers and a handful of gen-x'ers meant that my references weren't understood by those reading my text or hearing me lecture in a class. A friend of mine at my defence spoke up and said, "Fuck you, this is me" at my defence which summed it nicely up! This is the language we use, the language I chose to use, are you going to grammar me out of it? And I was subsequently grammar'd out of it. My slang writing in my thesis was picked apart and I was pressured to change it. When I expressed concern that I wanted it to sound youthful and read like a zine the response was, "You can't work in the idea that this is an anthology or a zine because it's getting you a master's degree and ultimately you are choosing a master's degree." So much for integration.

4. The feminist academia hasn't figured out where it stands on race/racism and coming up against that confusion and the missteps that I took was a scary thing. I was pretty much accused of being racist at my thesis defence and I definitely felt like I was being lambasted out of left field: how come no one in the four years of my being in grad school (learning and seeking guidance from professors and texts) suggested what I was tackling was way more problematic than I conceived it to be? And why did no one steer me in the direction of doing it right or better? By choosing to trust feminism (and third-wave feminism to boot) by focusing on my experiences as being my authority on my experience (a very feministy thing!) meant that I was not just alienating everyone else, but specifically alienating anyone who the Academy considered as racialized. Which kind of surprised me. The texts and experiences I was using to build my argument and create "change" were just as outdated as the Academy and didn't push me as much as I needed.

And I'm surprised, even now, that I felt like I trusted the feminist academia, maybe because they were "just like me!" I felt like I was engaging in forward discussions, but really women's studies, no matter where it is, relies on the same outdated texts and theories that everyone else does: it's so institutionalized. The reason that no one told me is because no one really knows! I felt like I was paying this university to TEACH me something important and something useful about my area of study, about feminism, how to be a good feminist. I thought I was teaching the university something about being forward thinking, but the forwardness I was proposing wasn't enough, and that's why I felt blindsided: what mattered to me wasn't the right thing to care about. And I get it! My feelings aren't even hurt! I know that the language I was using was not inclusive of everyone's feminisms (see my above discussion of the use of the words, "us" "our", etc) and I'm writing it this way since I want to be honest and tell you that I made mistakes. I am complicit in all of this.

Even when I went away and did additional research on how third-wave feminism reacts to race and difference in texts, the academic response was muddled and confused. What I've learned from that experience is that just stating, "I'm white, I know that I'm white, and this sounds white" wasn't enough. I feel that the "F"eminism I had come into contact with even in my community hadn't prepared me to be savvy in terms of anti-oppression work. I was surprised to find out that I was expected to write about someone's experience that wasn't mine to make my thesis supposedly more "inclusive" of other voices. And I struggled because third-wave feminism had set me up to believe that I can't just pick a racialized group of feminists and write about "them" in my thesis to make my feminism "more inclusive" because someone feels "bad" about how much space they're taking up. That's appropriation! And while I still find this confusing and don't want to appropriate anyone else's resistance or oppression, especially in the situation of me using someone else's experience as a "study" in the academy, I felt that there wasn't enough space given to me to make mistakes in the academy and learn how to do it "right" there. SO MUDDY! SO MESSY!

The reason I didn't get any concrete guidance on this is because the Academy hasn't figured it out yet, the Academy wasn't/isn't made for opening itself up to questioning, difference, change, isms, etc, and people who are interested in opposing don't want to talk about RACE for fear of saying something wrong and being labelled as racist (by other "white" people). Only by moving through my hang ups (and the hang ups of others who listened to me) about the words I/they use(d) and my fear of making mistakes could I have had truly hard discussions about race and racism. And then maybe through my experience future students or current faculty could have picked up some strategies of their own and then one day, maybe then the halls of the ivory towers will be more welcoming and less white-washed. But, I feel like this space wasn't available, and it's just whiny of me, a white person to say, "there's not enough space for me to figure out how I'm being racist!"

5. You can't assume that all women in the Academy are your friends, your feministy cohorts, or even your sisters in solidarity. The minute you do some of them will turn around and burn you...or at least eat you alive in an attempt to get above you. Even professors.

6. Young "third-wave" feminists (focus: pop-culture) and older "second-wave" feminists (focus: equal work for equal pay, birth control, 1970s-80s porn wars) are textually opposed to each other in the Academy. And these texts, most often written by second-wave feminists, tend to blame the younger feminists for all the strife. Even though I developed positive relationships with second-wave feminist academics, the third-wave is still blamed for creating the divide between the old battle axes of feminism and the young ones. And then the second wavers continue to turn around and write in their tenured journal publications that the third-wave continues to not exist and that young feminists and the feminisms used don't exist because my parts don't look like your parts. This is because the second-wave feminist academic structure doesn't have a way to recognize the work of young feminists as "real" feminism. I'm pretty sure this is because there are so few young feminists in graduate school doing new things, doing different things, being loud and quiet and questioning and resisting the prescribed outcomes for your time in Academia.

***

And to all of this I say, BOO! Even though my fantasy was to have the Academy stand back and say, "Yes! Yes! we've been doing this all wrong the whole time! Young people have valuable things to say! How could we have been so remiss!?", at the end of the whole long experience I've decided that I don't care. I don't need the Academy to be OK with my feminism, with young feminism, or with me saying "fuck" in a lecture. I kind of want to be left alone, to throw on my sneakers, and hit the street, the internet, the community and be a radical, be a feminist, and be myself.

* * *

Diandra Jurkic-Walls, aka ohsweetie, *is a crafter and radical third-wave feminist. Currently based on Vancouver Island, British Columbia Diandra can be found feministing in her community, watching every episode of* Gossip Girl, *raising her new baby, and knitting up a storm.*

JOCELYN FORMSMA

My Journey to Indigenous Feminism

The first feminist I ever met was a man. He was in his early 30s from Quebec and I was blown away when he casually uttered the words "I'm a feminist" in conversation. Before that, I admit that I had held many of the common stereotypes about feminists, namely that they were man-hating, bra-burning, middle-class white women that got offended at everything. It never occurred to me that a feminist could be a man, or happy, or poor or an Indigenous person. I certainly never thought that I was or could be a feminist.

I grew up in a middle class family and we had what we needed plus a little extra every now and then, so we were never deprived of basic necessities. I played sports in my small rural town and got involved in school, so I always felt as though I was a part of the community I lived in. I attended traditional ceremonies, so I was taught at an early age to value myself as a woman and received teachings about the special and powerful role women have in a community. Many of the organizations I volunteered with and worked for had women in both elected and hired leadership positions, many of these women became my mentors. Additionally, I was surrounded by strong female role models on both my mother and father's sides of my family.

Generally, I have gone through life oblivious to the fact that being a woman anywhere else in the country or the world may have affected my life experiences.

As I grew and learned more about the history of Canada and feminism, I began to realize that the values that had been instilled in me from a young age were not automatically the broader societal truth. When I was first introduced to the concept of feminism, I did not connect with some of the messages of feminism, specifically that women had always been oppressed and that the work of a feminist was to get women an equal piece of the pie or create a whole new pie altogether because I had taken the idea of women's equality for granted. I had no reason to think that there was nothing a woman could not do or could not achieve simply because she was a woman. My familial, cultural and personal experiences had made me think the opposite, that women were inherently strong and were the natural leaders within the family and the community. I have since learned that women from many different backgrounds still face many institutional and societal barriers and that a lot of the history of feminism has been written without the recognition that not all women were allowed to participate in the various women's movement "waves" and evolution of feminist theories. Many of the women that have been left behind by feminism have been Indigenous women.

I read a book by Devon Abbott Mihesuah called *Indigenous American Women* and I immediately connected with the book's content. This was a book written by an Indigenous woman talking about diversity of the Indigenous woman's experience. She outlined the many ways that Indigenous women were different, but also the many ways Indigenous women are the same. I was elated to see that someone else had thought of the same questions and concerns I had as I tried to understand exactly what it means to be an Indigenous woman. Page by page, I found myself soaking in every word and experienced an entire paradigm shift in thinking about the differences between feminists and Indigenous feminists.

While feminism was something I had studied in university, Indigenous feminism was something I had lived. Although Indigenous people are diverse in geography, language, culture and experience, the connection is often a common history.

Through first contact with Europeans, the fur trade, treaty making, establishment of the Indian Act, creation of the child welfare system, and many of today's continuing policies, the strong role women always had in social, political, economic and cultural governance was diminished — diminished, but never erased.

As Devon Mihesuah explains in her book, while feminists are concerned with the situation of women, *Indigenous* feminists are concerned with the situation of an *entire community*. Most, if not all, Indigenous feminists share the common goals of restoration. The goals of restoration can come in many forms, of language, culture, traditional roles, balance amongst the sexes and balance amongst the generations. That is also to say, restoration with the intention of moving forward. There has been no Indigenous feminist that I have met who wasn't working towards the goal of restoration in one way or another.

To me, Indigenous feminism is a way of practicing the values that I have been taught. Identifying as an Indigenous feminist means, without explicitly stating, that I believe in the inherent strength of women. It means that I not only am aware of and understand some of the historical and contemporary challenges and barriers that affect Indigenous women but also can appreciate that not all Indigenous women experience those same challenges and barriers in the same way or even at all. As an Indigenous feminist, I believe in the restoration of balance between and amongst the genders and the sexes and Indigenous feminism is where I find myself able to connect and commit to action.

For years, I couldn't admit to being a feminist because I felt as though I was placing a label on myself. I felt that I would have to explain or qualify that statement to make people feel more at ease with it. At first, I was hesitant to label myself as an Indigenous feminist, but as a friend once said "Instead of qualifying the feminist label by stating what you are not, state what you are and broaden the circle of what a feminist could be". So, I thank that man from Quebec for being the first step in my journey towards Indigenous feminism and I thank everyone in between, namely my family, colleagues and mentors, that helped me to learn more about who I am and helped shape what I believe. I still have a long way to go on this journey, but I am happy and I am an Indigenous feminist.

* * *

Jocelyn Formsma *is a member of the Moose Cree First Nation and currently lives in Ottawa, ON. She has been involved in children's rights and youth engagement for the last 10 years. Jocelyn was involved with the Friendship Centre Movement for a number of years at the local, regional and national levels as a board member and youth representative. She was the recipient of the inaugural Canadian Coalition on the Rights of Children's Child's Rights Award in 2009. Jocelyn is currently completing her Bachelor of Public Administration at the University of Ottawa. She also volunteers with the Nishnawbe Aski Nation, Chiefs of Ontario, is a co-host for a weekly community radio show, and has begun fiction writing and short filmmaking.*

KRYSTA WILLIAMS and ASHLING LIGATE

This Shit Is Real
Deconstructing dialogue in feminist education

Talking our talk

We have the privilege of time and education to talk about things like decolonization and feminism and cupcakes taking over the world. We also have the privilege to be comfortable in academic spaces and feel entitled to speak as feminists. Making sense of how theory applies to our lived experiences is what we talk about on a daily basis. We want to share with you these conversations, since they have meant a lot to both of us. But first, a small introduction about our experiences as students trying to deconstruct academia and feminism...

Krysta: So I have an undergrad degree from the University of Waterloo. One of my majors was psychology, and I had many interesting classmates. A friend of mine was also in the program with me and we were some of the few Native students in that program; some of the only ones it felt like. One day, my friend was on MSN (an online chat program) trying to get some help for an assignment that was due the next day. She noticed a classmate of ours, who was aware of who we were, had posted a rather striking message as their screen name. "Aboriginal students are more likely to commit suicide than go to university", or something like that. My friend called me, unsure of what to do, if anything. I decided to rant on the phone for half an hour about how offensive, racist and inappropriate, not to mention disrespectful, that comment was. But we had to sit with them in class and do group work together. I decided not to speak to them, but my friend, decided to try and explain why those actions were offensive. The person who posted it thought they were doing us a favor, that suicide was an "issue" that people needed to be informed about! I accidentally ran into them a few weeks later in the psychology labs and there was an attempted apology (the kind that comes with a justification). I confronted them and tried to explain, as nicely as I could, that it was racist. That our communities are beautiful and doing what we can to grapple with our struggles. We are not only a statistic and those numbers do not always reflect the reality that we face every day.

Ashling: I left home when I was sixteen to attend a college in the United States — the United World College of the American West, which is part of an international system of schools that "use education as a force to unite peoples, cultures and nations for peace and a sustainable future." My years there were incredible but I also had some very disheartening and challenging experiences, as would be expected when 200 youths from over 90 different "nationalities" are put on the side of an isolated mountain and told to work out their shit. I would fly home to Ontario for winter solstice every year to reconnect with family and friends. During one of these trips I met my mother's new partner for the first time. We went out to a sushi restaurant to join the rest of the white diners seeking an 'authentic' Japanese meal. (I guess we were all sick of eating over-cooked green beans and Yorkshire Pudding.) My mother's partner — let's call him Bob — ranted to me between bites of barbecued eel that he was sick of seeing his hard-earned dollars being given to "[insert racial slur] Indians." Once I had recovered from choking on my soy bean, I told him in the most composed voice I could muster that it is important that we, as "white" folks, understand what unearned privileges we are afforded. The Canadian government depends on institutionalized racism: the Indian Act, the reserve system, and intrapersonal stereotypes are all tools that serve to naturalize whiteness, to render it invisible. Bob and I tiptoed around each other for a few minutes before calling it a night and driving home in the impossible silence of his hybrid Lexus.

Krysta: I met Ashling while she worked for the Waterloo Public Interest Research Group (WPIRG) of which I am a board member. WPIRG was one of the few spaces on campus I felt remotely safe. As an organization with a mandate to address social and environmental justice, conversations about "controversial" topics were welcomes. I quickly realized that her analysis of oppression was bang on with mine and we had many amazing discussions about racism on campus, colonization and whiteness. I shared with her many stories about my frustrations with our campus' "diversity" campaign and the lack of support for critical thinking from professors. I had also finally met someone who took seriously the role of Indigenous ally (someone who supports you, and also challenges their own complicity in the system that produce harm). I shared with her a lot of my experiences working with Aboriginal Services on campus and what it was like to be a Native student at the University of Waterloo. (Which wasn't all angst and rage, we had a small tight-knit community that was very supportive and I learned how to make fry bread/bannock eight different ways!).

Ashling: I really appreciate that Krysta and I, in addition to enjoying hilarious times as bosom buddies, are able to learn from each other in non-tokenizing and real ways. As an academic in Women's Studies, I often feel as though I am required to climb mountains in order to have my peer-to-peer learning experiences recognized and appreciated as legitimate and grounded sources of knowledge. Why are oral histories labelled as "radical" sources? From my perspective there is nothing radical about honouring people's truths, honouring my own truth. I should be able to cite a conversation I have with Krysta in a paper focused on decolonization, just as I should be able to draw upon my own lived experiences of homophobia in a seminar course on Feminist Theory. Dialogue is one of the most important and powerful tools we have at our disposal, especially in an academic context.

Krysta: I whole-heartedly agree! * high five * This is also why we wanted to create this piece, so people could see good and bad (and sometimes ugly) examples of dialogue from our lived experiences and between us now! We, as feminists, as people who experience different forms of oppression, as friends, want to show the world that talking about injustice in a good way is possible, it's happening and it's necessary!

Ashling: I especially want this to happen in classrooms, in hallways, where students are asked to engage with issues of resource distribution, gendered violence, and international development. There is a lack of urgency in academia to link the anecdotal stories and statistics in our readings to a real need to resist and dismantle patriarchal and [neo]colonial structures of oppression. For example, when I see a statistic in my textbook about violence against Native women in Canada, I need to understand that these numbers are real. I need to discuss with my (mostly white) peers what these numbers actually mean in relation to sexual violence, a central topic in Women's Studies. In my experiences, I've been able to see those links most clearly through dialogue not only with peers and professors but also with my neighbour, aunt, and grocer. The following tips and tricks are relevant tools to everyone but we know that the language of "oppression, injustice and discrimination" assume a particular reader, someone who is already engaged with some form of "activism".

Krysta: So take your anti-oppression training (if you have had or heard of any) with a chunk of salt and instead we challenge you to see and place yourself in these pages. We challenge you to enact what you read here or to envision your own strategies if what we offer does not work for you. It is my hope that this will not be taken as a judgement of character but a gesture of love and hope. For me, challenging the stereotypical ideas and thoughts I had about Native people was the hardest part. It was ingrained in me, my education and the media I consumed. I also felt like a "bad Indian" for not knowing about my culture, language etc. These are lessons learned the hard way from peers, friends, Elders, and random strangers. It is not easy, nor should it be. It is uncomfortable, and sometimes it hurts. But that's how you know you're learning, and what you chose not to act on now, might hurt more in the future.

Thoughts on being radically traditional from Krysta

I personally struggle a lot with my love/hate relationships with language. I personally love words in general, but have a lot of problems with English despite the fact that it is my first language. It seems so arbitrary and subjective. It also does not allow me to express the very distinct and varying terms of reference that we have as Aboriginal people. So when I say "traditional", I am talking about teachings and stuff I have learned from Elders and teachers in my life. But even then, who gets to define "traditional"? Where does it start or end? Our cultures are alive, adapting and changing every day. When I talk about being "socially progressive" or "radical" is can mean many things. Sometimes it is a tongue-in-cheek way of poking fun at the ways mainstream culture tries to be different or better. Gender equality may be a "radical" concept to some people, but to me, it is tradition. Having a "traditional" wedding would mean very different things depending on who you are talking to. So to me, being traditional IS radical and having dialogue about difficult things IS radical, because it goes against every push from the system to be a quiet, stoic "Indian".

Walking the walk

The following was constructed based on a series of conversations between Krysta and Ashling. The writing was collaborative, with space and responsibilities shared equally.

Some folks in academia like to call our struggles "interesting" and theorize about our lived experiences. They churn out 40 page long papers on the shit we live with every single day and never ask us what it actually feels like. Nor do they bother to ask what our different communities are already doing to survive, thrive and reclaim. Once in a blue moon someone will stare at us, mouth agape, and proclaim that they are so incredibly sorry for our experiences of oppression.

We do not want to hear apologies. We do not want to be placed in a glass jar and used as fodder for a purposeless case study. We do not want to do this to others.

We want to share our lived experiences with those who are ready and open to listen without judgement or reacting defensively. We want to have our peer-to-peer education recognized as a valid academic pursuit. Sometimes all we want is acknowledgement and silence.

If you are a student at a university, there are significant barriers that are presented if you are willing to take on the responsibility of integrating academics with your life outside of the classroom. Rarely is dialogue recognized as a form of education, even in so-called 'feminist' spaces, such as Women's Studies Departments. When students try to seek out opportunities to learn from other human beings, the tools needed to support that process are not made available.

If you are not a student in a university, please email us and let us know what it's like out there. It is equally difficult to have these conversations and dialogues with peers, friends and family. It's time consuming, sometimes emotionally draining. Frankly, sometimes we are too busy dealing with this stuff and surviving, that we don't have the resources to sit and think about it and write a paper.

When the system cannot deliver (which is too often), one option we may have is to create our own realities within our present circumstances. We would like to share with our peers some tips and tricks on how to engage in respectful and meaningful peer-to-peer feminist education about oppression. We offer these insights, opinions and suggestions as our own unique selves who have experienced both privilege and oppression in different situations. As you read along, we encourage you to actively respond to what is written here on these pages: if something doesn't fit with you, leave it and move on.

We, Krysta and Ashling, worked in collaboration to create this resource and were able to take the time to discuss each point as it related to our own lives. During our journeys as colleagues, peers, and friends, we have been able to learn from each other by building trust and creating safer spaces. In this written medium we are sometimes limited in our abilities to adequately express ourselves (the colonizers words in English are tragically uninspiring). We are also limited by the inescapable barrier between 'author' and 'reader': we cannot listen to and acknowledge your stories, meet your eyes or share physical space. We can, however, hope that you will find some truth in what we offer and will take the risk to try these tips in your spaces of learning.

We see this list as both treatment and prevention. Treatment for those academics we have been harmed by, directly and indirectly. There is a joke about how every Native community has its own anthropologist, though its very funny so much as true. To those academics who continue to take knowledge from our communities and lives in order to become highly paid "experts", this is for you. But it is also prevention, for those thinking about post-secondary or already there. We even hope this can be adapted for anyone wanting to have an honest conversation — but maybe that's too ambitious. Either way, you will ultimately decide whether this is relevant to you, and how you will chose to use this list.

TIP 1: Challenge yourself to translate academic theory into personal lived experiences from yourself, your communities, and others. Make it real.

DON'T tell me my struggle/fight/cause/issue is "like, really interesting". I don't give a shit that it's interesting. It's killing me.

DO your homework! Read books, articles by people that are part of the community you are learning about.

DON'T offer sympathy as your only reaction. Do not feel sorry, feel responsible.

DO acknowledge that every issue is someone's lived experience and open yourself to empathize with their pain and struggles without being creepy. Be real.

Ashling: As a women's studies major, I spend a great deal of my time in seminar meetings and am encouraged to engage with the assigned readings in discussion with my peers. I bring myself — my stories, my experiences, my perspective — to these discussions because that is part of what it means to me to live my feminism: it encourages me to intertwine my academics with my lived understandings of reality. I'll offer stories about what it is like to live in the margins of hetero/homosexual binaries, what it feels like to sit in a lecture hall of 200 people and have the professor tell me that I need to "tolerate the gays on campus." Usually I receive blank stares from the folks around the table, who then quickly avert their eyes to the assigned pages on identity politics, clearly most comfortable with theoretical conceptions of identity politics. Once in a while, someone will paraphrase my words and say that what I experience is "tragic proof" that the patriarchy is still intact. While the last part of that statement is true, I am not an anecdote to fuel your misdirected rage. I am not a side issue to be relegated to the final chapter in your intro textbook. My stories are real and I live them every day.

> **TIP 2: Reflect on how you have benefited, supported, or are complicit in a system that oppresses others (if you are coming from a place of privilege).**
>
> DON'T pretend that you are separate from systems of oppression.
>
> DO recognize that you profit in some ways off of other's oppressions. If you are experiencing one form of oppression, you can still benefit from the oppression of others. For example, Ashling is a queer woman and has experienced queer-phobia but continues to profit from the legacies and current realities of slavery.

Ashling: For example, until a few months ago I had no idea that there had ever been black slaves in Canada: a massive part of the history of the creation of this colony that was conveniently omitted from any of my high school textbooks. I was floored (though perhaps it shouldn't have been so surprising) to learn that the colonies on the East Coast were built by black slaves, who were brutalized and later driven out of the cities by the whites. The destruction of Africville, a community of black families in Nova Scotia, by the white government in the 1960's was glossed over as a project of [forced] "relocation" and "urban renewal." (Check out the website www.africville.ca for more information.) And I thought that Nova Scotia "belonged" to white fishermen…

Krysta: I work really hard every day to try and decolonize, which is a constant, ongoing process. I think a lot of people need to get real about this. Racism isn't an evil monster living under the bed. It's a system that upholds white supremacy in this land and gives unearned privilege to a lot of people. That's not a two sided debate, it's just fact.

> **TIP 3: Make the time to integrate what you have been made aware of into your perspective/life. Take time to think, process, read and talk to people in order to work through potentially difficult material. Recognize this as a process of learning, not just a onetime experience.**
>
> DON'T assume that no one is, or has taken action on something, just because it is new to you. Find out how you can support causes/ issues you care about, without "spearheading" another initiative that might drive attention away from community based projects.
>
> DO understand that feminist education, and learning about oppression is a life long journey. The more I (Krysta) learn about my own history, the more and more I realize how much there is that I don't know.

Krysta: Learning about residential schools where Aboriginal children were forcibly removed from their families and communities, forced to unlearn everything they had ever known, and most experiencing multiple forms of violence and abuse in the process, is really overwhelming. Seeing films or meeting Survivors is real and painful. It is very easy to reject this knowledge with a sweeping statement about how it's all history now and the horrors are over. Or think that everyone's experiences were awful and that this system was created by evil people with the intention to kill. If we refuse to recognize that the current "social worker" mentality is still very close to the mentality that created residential schools, we will simply see history repeated. And I believe we are with the current lived realities of First Nations children "in care". Please realize that good intentions are simply not enough to do the hard work to challenge and reconstruct these systems of power.

> **TIP 4: Recognize that despite everything, communities that are labelled as "oppressed" or are struggling, are still vibrant, alive and thriving in whatever ways they can.**

DON'T think that we are incapable of producing knowledge, or are too busy with living that we don't think about art, music, or other "privileged" topics of thought.

DO seek out artists, media makers and shakers, activists, authors*, not only as a way to learn, but also as a concrete means of supporting a community.

*Note: There is a huge problem with "outside" authors appropriating and reproducing knowledge from particular communities, and gaining a lot profit from it. For example, white anthropologists are still considered "experts" on communities to which they do not belong. But Native people who write about their communities, are considered "biased". This is racism.

Ashling: While I was studying as an undergrad at the University of Victoria on Lekwungen territory, I was very fortunate to be able to take a number of classes with Christine Welsh, who is a deservedly celebrated and incredibly passionate Métis filmmaker. She introduced me to the vast world of Indigenous women's filmmaking. In our classes, we would discuss the ways that we were personally moved by each film and share which ways we were going to translate our learning into our everyday actions. For my final assignment in one of Christine's classes on "Decolonizing the Screen" I compiled a guide to engaging with Indigenous film specifically for folks like myself who wish to self-educate through media and knowledge created by those who work from lived experience. From productions of international fame like Atanarjuat (Igloolik Isuma Productions, 2000) to gems that are out of circulation like Deep Inside Clint Star (NFB, 1999), the world of Indigenous film is beautifully complex and layered and is a great source for learning.

Krysta: This is a prime example of my love/hate relationship with feminism. There is so much knowledge out there attributed to white western feminists! When I started learning about "academic feminism" (which was different than my lived experience around amazingly strong women) I was like, "Wait a minute, weren't we doing this like 500 years ago?!". Yes, yes we ARE. There are many phenomenal Indigenous feminists that deserve just as much (if not more) love and recognition as your Women's Studies 101 writers.

Question for Ashling from Krysta: I am curious about the guide you mentioned. What does it mean for you when you needed to create a guide to "translate" what Indigenous people were saying so that others could learn and benefit? Do you see this as maybe playing into the *note that I brought up above?

Ashling: Thanks for challenging me. The purpose of creating a "guide" for white folks was two-fold. Firstly, I wanted to compile a list of films made mostly by Indigenous women because I think that their artistry should be known and appreciated. Secondly, I wanted to record the resources that my peers and I had compiled during Christine Welsh's classes that supported our viewings in specific historical and cultural contexts. For example, one of the films in the guide is Alanis Obomsawin's Kanehsatake: 250 Years of Resistance and one of the supporting viewing resources listed is Lee Maracle's book *Bobbi Lee: Indian Rebel*. With all that said, I am still chewing over your question and want to keep this in the back of my mind, as I think there's more here that I'm not understanding or recognizing yet.

TIP 5: Dialogue is radical. Talking about social justice in a way that doesn't prescribe ownership to you, is one way of being a true ALLY. Talking to your family about the history of residential schools for example can be more radical than putting up posters, wearing a button or hosting a rally.

DO be ready to take on "menial" tasks for communities you are trying to "ally" with.

DO shut up as a way of supporting a community and making space for frequently unheard voices.

DO simply ASK what needs to be done, and do it, no questions asked. DON'T expect ally work to be easy or glamorous. Doing the dishes can be extremely helpful!

DO your homework. again. always.

Krysta: Believe it or not, allyship can go really, really wrong. There are too many examples of well meaning "radical" groups wanting to "help" at demonstrations that Native communities are leading. This can lead to increased police brutality and violence against Native people, once those demonstrators have riled everyone up and left.

Tying it all together

We have no neat conclusion to offer you. Instead, we leave you with an open 'ending' in the hopes that the words filling these pages will not remain stagnant. They came from movement and out of reality — of being in dialogue with each other. The written word offers us a moment to pause, reflect, and record but its purpose is only realized in pairing with action. Now it's your turn to reflect on what we've shared and see how it may fit into your own life.

* * *

Krysta Williams is an Indigenous Feminist and Turtle clan from Moravian of the Thames First Nation. She is a traditional singer and drummer, learning songs and teachings from the many amazing women in Kitchener-Waterloo, Ontario. Krysta is the Lead Youth Advocate at the Native Youth Sexual Health Network, with a degree in Psychology and Spanish and Latin American Studies from the University of Waterloo. She is currently on the board of directors for the Waterloo Public Interest Research Group (WPIRG) - a social and environmental justice organization for and by students and community members. She is passionate about food justice, Indigenous self-determination and healing our relationship with the land.

Ashling Ligate is a queer ciswoman ("cis" — gender is same as sex assigned at birth) who was raised as a white person on the lands of the Six Nations of the Grand River territory. She is still growing into the responsibilities that come with identifying as a critical feminist. She is a community-focused artist whose passions include living simply and using theatre to address oppression and incite social change. She is currently finishing her undergraduate degree in Women's Studies at the University of Waterloo. She is also the Public Educator at the Sexual Assault Support Centre of Waterloo Region, which is a feminist non-profit that works to end sexual violence against women and children.

LISA MANTIA

Finding Our Voice in the Mainstream Media Madness

"**M**edia" is often said to be methods of communicating data and information, be it by television, internet, print, radio or others. Mass media is when these diverse forms are consolidated to control large portions of the outlets. The danger of this is that it limits the difference of ideas, filtering anything not in sync with the standard view (which is of course white, middle-upper class, capitalist, able-bodied, etc) of the business. Feminists have always had a hard time being represented in the mainstream (and an even harder time being represented positively). I believe that changing the media from the grassroots is vital for the evolution of feminist ideas because we need to have an accessible media to inform, discuss, and debate.

The relationship between media literacy in education and feminism doesn't get the attention it deserves, mainly because our media doesn't cover it. Oh the irony. But I suppose the reason is the vast complexity of it all. I mean, what is feminism in the first place? There's a different feminism for every person that identifies as a feminist, right? And what is the media? Is it any avenue to digest and portray ones ideas to the world? Going on that definition it can certainly have infinite avenues.

In my opinion, what's missing today is the lack of under-standing people have of our current media machine and how it greatly affects people's views. You see, it's not that the main-stream constantly lies outright (although sure, they do some-times). It's the lack of broad discussion. Some issues are simply too complex to understand after one line about it on the TV. For example when the news reports that there will be "minor budg-et cuts", what does that really mean in actuality? How will it affect social services? Consider these statistics: 35% of women who live on their own live in poverty — and this number rises to 41.5% for women over 65[1] — regardless of whether they are sin-gle, divorced or widowed. So how on earth can we try to analyse the budget without looking at the many layers of the issues?

Public opinion (or people's perceptions of public opinion) is monopolized in the media to focus on the one big world issue. The current climate is to shift people's view to centre on a "sexy" issue. Whether it's a perceived revolution or mass violence per-petrated by so-called "religious extremism", it is always por-trayed just enough for people to get petrified, then stereotypical-ly bigoted about the people involved and never long enough to know the history behind the situation or the future impacts of the people involved. This distorts the message and the responsi-bility of journalism, which is to effectively critique a situation so people are informed.

Feminist education can give us room to develop our social jus-tice based ideas. but we need a tool to bring these thoughts and ideas to action, and the media is a vital one. The consolidation of the media has pushed out dissenting voices, and has left us with a "one size fits all" approach to reporting. Fewer and fewer jour-nalists are reporting on issues from the actual sources them-selves. The removal of the journalists from the story source not only makes an in-depth report more difficult to obtain, but it also hinders the responsibility of the journalist to correct inac-curacies in their reporting. When local people are doing the reporting, community pressure of accuracy and follow up are much greater because of the direct access to the reporter. With community based reporting, we can increase awareness of the reporter and their sources.

Many feminists have been calling for an analysis of complex issues and how they all intersect with one another. So how do we start the discussion and change the media machine? Can we change it? Why does it need to be changed? There are many great alternative information sources in zines, blogs, and websites etc. But are these outlets truly accessible? The information they provide must be accessible so it can reflect the difference of opinions of society. Many media outlets require money to purchase newspapers, television sets, etc. Also with several "free" sources, such as the internet, it requires investments in computers and internet service.

We look to independent media to bring a democratic voice to the discussion, but it is not without its faults. Some alternative outlets cater to the same crowd who write and read it continually, and it has difficulty connecting to communities outside the one producing it. The large disparity between corporate media funding and independent media make it impossible to have the independent message in the view of the public at large. Topical issues push out other vital issues in the mainstream, but these sexy topics also push out important issues from independent sources too. If we are vying for any kind of major political feminist shift, from decriminalizing sex work to comprehensive reproductive health education in the public system, we will need to have access to the general public through the mainstream if we want an immediate push in public opinion.

Control of the media is probably the single most influential aspect of any power pursuit. It's always in somebody's interest to alter our perception of what is important. Take for example the Canadian government spending billions of dollars on war machines and cutting funding to many social services, including women's shelters, within the same year. Why was this not heavily criticized in the media? But yet the connection of the removal of money from social services to the increased military spending in the mainstream never happened. Why has there been little criticism of the change in funding? Who benefits from this?

The powers that be gain from an ignorant public; one that doesn't question but just *does*. There are many great journalists in Canadian and world media, but there's also a systematic problem with what and how things are reported, and who gets to report them in the first place. This is where feminism must step up and challenge the status quo. How can feminism do this? Where's the intersectionality of the issues? Where is the discussion of how the issues are so deeply entrenched with one another? How can there be no mainstream coverage when hundreds of Indigenous women go missing and are being murdered, yet there is usually non-stop analysis when a white girl goes missing?

Many people don't like feeling uncomfortable and these are very uncomfortable questions I'm asking, but they must be asked. We must support people to be critical of their perceptions of reality by sharing tools and resources to do so. We must talk to people in the kitchen, at the market, on the streets and change the culture. We need to bring the debate and discourse to the masses because if we don't, it will be left to the singleminded mass media. We have to give people the tools to understand where the information they receive comes from (who owns it) and what bias it has. Everyone has a bias; but knowing where it comes from helps to frame why they believe certain things. Public opinion is usually shaped by the big box media outlets. Although independent media is vital, change within the mainstream is imperative, but it will not change overnight. What's important is that we empower the next generation of people to not be afraid to question mainstream opinion and disagree with the pack. Most importantly we've got to support our next generations to make noise for the things they believe in.

> **Many people don't like feeling uncomfortable and these are very uncomfortable questions I'm asking, but they must be asked.**

There are never only two solutions for an issue. With so much complexity in a single event, it is ridiculous that the current media trend is to give us less and less analysis. For example, a common tactic is to make the message or the debate shrivel down to a sound bite between who's traveling where and who's wearing what. What I'm suggesting is not about limiting entertainment information or the fluff, but to inform our youth and up-and-coming generations of their right to media literacy and intake to reflect our multilayered reality. We need to bring debate into the news that includes all people and life experiences. We have to create a reality that tells the next generation of youth that they do have the power to change the course of history, because they do.

People underestimate the power of the media. It can create a culture of war or of peace. It can distract us from the real issues. It can blind us with shiny things as the world crumbles. Media is power. We can expose corruption with it. We can educate to link issues like reproductive justice and climate justice. Right now we live in a manufactured state of terror where ignorance, fear and hatred prevail. Through sharing our lived experiences and individual opinions and ideas, even when they contrast starkly with each other, we can begin to discuss the difficult. We need to know, teach and feel comfortable with that fact that there is rarely a right decision, but there is always a better one. Our world's problems are too complicated for only one or two sound bites to explain.

So how do we educate about the media? The answers are limitless. We can start by changing the curriculum to have media literacy classes in all different forms. We can make independent media more accessible to youth. We can encourage youth to create their own media. We can create a classroom that encourages debate and discussions about local and world issues. We can trust youth and know that they are more than capable to discuss and debate issues we are always told only adults would understand. We need a more comprehensive media to work with not just youth but with our entire population to create a realm of discussion and debate. Only with honest dialogue and critical thinking will we start to create a fairer world.

* * *

Lisa Mantia is a Toronto-based activist working for economic justice. She discovered it is very hard to find justice-based debates and discussions about economics in the mainstream media.

ENDNOTES

[1] "Women and Poverty"; Women's Legal Education and Action Fund document; http://www.leaf.ca/education/documents/EdHO_Women_Poverty.pdf.

KATE KLEIN

On Learning How *Not* to Be An Asshole Academic Feminist

I can't remember my Big Feminist Lightbulb Moment™. You know the one people talk about, where all of a sudden one day something opens your eyes to all the injustices this world has to offer and your mind explodes and your consciousness is raised and your life is forever changed, because — let's be honest — you couldn't close your eyes again even if you wanted to. I don't think it happened like that for me.

The development of my feminist critical consciousness was slow, like a puzzle being assembled, piece by piece, moment by moment. Like, the moment where I realized how messed up it was that my high school sweetheart was actually advising me, in all honesty and with a genuine personal feeling of goodwill, to maybe hold back from remarking on how women are represented in action movies, in order to avoid alienating my guy friends who "just don't like to think about that stuff". Or the moment when I stopped feeling flattered by catcalls and started realizing how insignificant and vulnerable they really made me feel. Like the moment I understood how absolutely inseparable my gender was from the marginalization I was feeling as a newly-out queer person. Or the moment when I was staffing a booth on my university's campus and noticed almost every person walking into the "Presidents' Reunion" being held across from me was a white man in a suit. There was never one big, earth-shaking, life-altering moment, only a series of puzzle pieces being slowly but surely added to the square, ultimately shaping the picture of what it looks like to be a woman like me living in the many different contexts of my life.

If you'd asked me back when I was still figuring out the whole "feminism" thing, though, I would have told you that I came into it all rather suddenly, serendipitously, and entirely by accident. In my first year at university, I didn't do very many things outside of schoolwork and hanging out with friends. I had been a very involved person when I was in high school, and I was itching to find some sort of activity that would be both fun and challenging. Luckily, in the winter semester, I was walking around campus with two women from my residence floor, and we came across a poster calling all women at my school to audition for that year's production of Eve Ensler's *The Vagina Monologues*. The three of us made a pact to get brave and audition, and I saw it as an amazing opportunity to immerse myself in theatre again (which was a huge part of my life in high school), and to overcome some personal fears ("We have to talk about what??").

I look back fondly at the first time I did *The Vagina Monologues* as a time in my life when I learned the value of breaking down walls of silence, the value of righteous outrage, the value of being loud and a little risqué when that is the last thing that is expected of you, and most of all, the value of making female friends in an environment where loving, non-judgmental support is the norm. Since that year, I have done *The Vagina Monologues* three more times, twice more as an actor, and once as a director. Each time has been a drastically different experience. With four years of *VM* experience and a lot more anti-oppressive knowledge under my belt, I no longer hold *The Vagina Monologues* up as the ultimate beacon of hope for women everywhere. The show certainly has many problems, including but not limited to a transphobic implication that everyone who has a vagina is a woman and that everyone who is a woman has a vagina, a rampant heteronormativity, and a recent focus on women in the Global South that, by virtue of the nature of university spaces, ends up casting privileged white women as "sex slaves" in the Democratic Republic of the Congo, or Japanese comfort women, and perpetuating colonialist representations of non-Western women. But, it will always, nonetheless, hold a soft spot in my heart because of the role it played in my initial years.

After my first year with *The Vagina Monologues,* I was inspired to join the Women's Centre at my school and instantaneously felt intellectually inept. After finding my feminist voice in the words of Eve Ensler's play, this came as a shock to me; that feminism wasn't entirely about screaming taboo words and talking about empowerment was (oddly) not something I had planned for. I was intensely envious of my friends who were majoring in Women's Studies, Sociology, and Cultural Studies, who seemed to be getting what I perceived at the time to be all the important information presented to them on a shiny silver plate.

I was intensely envious of my friends who were majoring in Women's Studies, Sociology, and Cultural Studies, who seemed to be getting what I perceived at the time to be all the important information presented to them on a shiny silver plate.

The feminist lingo, the names of all the "big players" in feminism, the oh-so-elusive "intersectional feminist analysis". Even the subtle but pervasive (white hipster) feminist fashion sense was beyond my skill set. Learning about social justice never seemed to come as easily for me as it did for others. I struggled with feeling uneducated, ignorant, and boring, as though everybody who had politics I respected was speaking a language I couldn't begin to engage in.

Let me explain: I am a psychology student. I tell you this not because my field is a cherished part of my identity, but because it gives you an idea of where I'm coming from. Mainstream psychology, you see, is a black hole for social justice. Not only was a social justice analysis not taught in psychology, it was actively discouraged, under the pretense of "reducing bias" and "encouraging objectivity". Having my activist spirit virtually beaten out of me in the classroom (with a big textbook entitled "On Being a Scientist") forced me to find wishfully anti-oppressive spaces like the Women's Centre, but even in those spaces I felt a little odd. It's not that there were that many differences between the others and me; I was (then) a liberal feminist, I was white, I was a closeted queer (and therefore had an apparently standard sexuality), I was conventionally feminine, and interested in the right things (Body image, check. Gender stereotypes, check. Violence against women, check). I just wasn't a part of the Women's Studies "club", and it showed through in the words I chose and in my lack of "analysis". Meanwhile, across the country, women of colour, Aboriginal women, trans women, women with disabilities, and women with other intersecting identities and different "analyses" were facing social exclusion in mainstream Women's Centres because of many feminists' inability to see the need for anything beyond a feminist analysis.

All this time I had been envious of a set of tools that were, in reality, not only incomplete but, in many ways, oppressive; I would later need to look elsewhere in the hopes of gaining a richer understanding of the dynamics of racism, colonialism, cissexism, classism, ableism, and all the other systems of domination that a solely feminist analysis cannot hope to reflect and challenge. My problem was that because I was so steeped in "Women's Centre culture", and because of my privileged social location, I wasn't actually aware that I was missing these tools; while university feminist spaces often purport to promote anti-oppression, my experience has been that this is mostly all talk with very little concrete action to show for it. When a bunch of white women sit around decrying racism in a space where there are, suspiciously, no women of colour around to lead and shape that dialogue, it quickly becomes clear who the space is geared towards.

Today, I pride myself in being a self-taught feminist. I feel like a fraud sometimes for never having read any bell hooks or Judith Butler, but find joy in the fact that the "theorists" who have been the most influential for me are close friends, past and current lovers, and people I don't know who write blogs on the internet. My experience of coming into feminism in this way, backwards and upside down, greatly informs how I engage with the world, but is this experience (which, let's be honest, is only *slightly* unconventional) enough to call myself a feminist who is "not of the academy"?

Developing as a feminist in the context of a university Women's Centre, in a sense, prepared me well for being a "successful" professional feminist in the most superficial of senses; I finished my undergrad with a bevy of great experiences to put on my resume, the ability to cater my political messages to a variety of people, and the absurd ability to engage in personal reflection in the absence of any sort of outside critique. I am now well versed in the language that those women in my first year at the Women's Centre had. I've learned the ways of feminist university spaces, how to negotiate them, how to facilitate them, and how to lead them. I've gained the social capital to be respected and taken seriously in these spaces, and while I've still never taken a Women's Studies class in my life, the university is my home; while my feminism was never learned in the classroom, it, nonetheless, was gained in a space of intellectual elitism, class privilege, colonialism, and whiteness. Really and truly, I have become a part of the club that I felt so excluded from in the first place, and I don't like it. I reject the definitions of success that were taught to me in feminist university spaces, but simultaneously can't help but be drawn to them, and this is an ongoing tension for me.

Recently, I went on a date with somebody who decided that university wasn't for her partway through her formal education. We had nothing to talk about, not because we didn't have any chemistry, but because I couldn't think of anything to say to her that didn't make me sound like a school-obsessed snob. I began to panic: Am I so sheltered that I can't even manage to have a conversation with somebody who doesn't have a degree? Am I one of those self-obsessed white ladies who couldn't see her own privilege if it hit her in the face? Am I a part of the problem, not the solution? Am I destined never to have a dialogue with somebody that's not about practicum placements, syllabi, and departmental drama? I began to wonder: How can I call myself an anti-violence activist when there are people who have stories of terror and violation that go untold in the spaces I occupy because the language in which they express them is not one deemed acceptable by hegemonic academic elitism (aka: university snobbery)? How much more seriously are my own stories taken as an activist who operates within the academy, now that I know how to even pronounce the word "hegemony" and can pretend to know how to use it? Should we allow anti-violence, for example, to be shaped and framed within academic discursive spaces, or is that a form of violence in and of itself?

I still don't know the answers to these questions. What I do know is that there is currently a monumental gap between "the academy" and "the community" (whatever that is), with feelings of paternalistic disdain from one side and feelings of exasperated dismissal from the other. I feel somehow ungrateful for criticizing my university feminist grooming, since that's where I've learned everything I know (there and in "the blogosphere"), and especially because the ability to receive a university education is such a privilege, but how can I ever hope to be a true agent of social change if all I know how to do is engage with people like me in a university context?

My puzzle of feminist development isn't finished yet. I am still young, and I know that as long as I continue to seek out new opportunities, continue to step out of my comfort zone (which means leaving the university context for one single ever-loving moment) and continue to challenge myself and others, I will continue to have new moments of clarity, new moments where I feel a little closer to the truth of what it can mean to be a woman, and not just a woman "like me". I don't pretend that my own personal existential crisis is in any way new or groundbreaking; all I can hope for in the work that I do is to attempt to kick a couple of stones into that gap between the academy and the community and listen to them rattle around until they hit the bottom, hopefully contributing just a little bit to filling the gap.

I know now, after my experiences at university with the Women's Centre and *The Vagina Monologues* that an enormous part of my feminism is about relationships, allies, and community. I've learned that hope is nothing without people to be hopeful with, that the good fight isn't so great when you're doing it alone, that success is that much sweeter when it is achieved alongside and not on the backs of others, and that hardship is so much easier when you have somebody there to say, "*I know. I've been there.*" Those lessons *can't* be university-specific, they just can't be. Yes, that is the feminism that I have learned at school, but I hope that it's also a feminism that I can carry forward, one day, when I finally figure out how not to be an asshole academic feminist.

* * *

Kate Klein *is an artist/activist/academic who has a healthy appreciation for swear words, consensus decision-making, tattoos, and the Internet. She identifies with radical politics, and as a sex-positive queer feminist who works primarily with issues of body sovereignty.*